Belize

The Final Chapter

(Viva, Mexico! And Other Assorted Love Songs)

ALAN HEAD

PAGE PUBLISHING, INC.
New York, NY

First originally published by Page Publishing, Inc. 2018

ISBN 978-1-64214-676-9 (Paperback)
ISBN 978-1-64214-678-3 (Hardcover)
ISBN 978-1-64214-677-6 (Digital)

Printed in the United States of America

To my new best of friend and confidante, Olga Cervantes Lopez, who in so many ways saved me from a life of misery and despair. Here's to you, Olga. Cheers.

A New Country, A New Life

As the waning crescent moon gracefully slumbered in its final descent in the western sky, John gazed out the window facing west from the kitchen at the brilliantly lighted circular Aki grocery store signage in the forefront of a *rojo* and *amarillo* sunset. The letters were as such, as in lowercased. The sign, which was *rojo* with an *amarillo* trim and *blanco* lettering, except for the dot on the *i*, which was *amarillo*, was shouting out to anyone and everyone who once knew him, "*Aqui*, I'm here! See, in Chetumal, where the *dias* are long and hot but the *noches* are wonderfully *hermosa* and the people are too! I miss you all."

It was the day after July 4, 2016, and John had just moved into his new apartment in Chetumal on the northwest side of downtown, about two kilometers to the northeast of the airport. The apartment was capacious for a one-bedroom bungalow on the second story behind the many businesses lining San Salvador Avenue. The building was made of cinder blocks with a white masonry exterior and with one entry to the adjoining concrete courtyard and mezzanine above, one on the north side and one on the south side. Inside, there was a large *cocina* on the right, or west-facing side, a bath in the center, and a large bedroom, about twelve feet by twenty feet, on the left. The flooring was all tile with a *muy bonita verde* finish with *blanco* patterns sprinkled in. The tile was different in each of the three rooms as to the shade of green and style of the pieces.

The apartment was on the top level of the two-story white stone apartment building and was at the end of a cul-de-sac on the back side facing the Posada Inn to the south and was very private and quiet. Outside of the entry to John's apartment was a veranda overlooking the avenue, with a sink and washing area if one were so inclined to wash their own clothes. John swore to himself that he would never do that again. *Knock on wood*, John thought.

There were two apartments on the second story: his and the other on the front side, which was vacant at the time. It was secluded and quiet with the entire top level to himself. The outside upper level was encapsulated by the high second story walls of the business on the left, and the residence on the right, giving it the sense of being in a courtyard. Next to the residence to the east was a dentist office and to the west, Edgar's blended *frutas* shake shop.

Even though San Salvador Avenue was just a stone's throw from his apartment, one couldn't hear the traffic from the street due to the constant drone of the rotating fan in the kitchen. Across the street, there was a hair salon where Carla, whom he had met that morning and who was from Orange Walk, gave John a much-needed haircut. To the west was her father's late-night hamburger stand, and beyond their gated car entrance was a *lavanderia*, a Chinese restaurant, and cell phone accessories shop, and just across the encroaching and ending street from the north was a soccer field.

John had taken his clothes to be done at the *lavanderia*, which was unlike in Belize where he had handwashed his clothes and hung them on a line for drying. There were three *farmacias* on each of the three of four corners, either left or right. On the fourth corner, just east of John's apartment, a *farmacia* had shut down years before. The remaining stores were all open 24-7—which was odd, one might think. Most of the stores along the avenue were sparsely patronized, and most shut down for siesta time in the midafternoon. Carla minded her shop with meticulous care, constantly cleaning and sweeping or mopping her tiled floor when there were no customers, which was often the case. But it was her life and her salon, and she seemed happy in her life.

This would be the sixth home in the past seven years for John and Molly, and this one he felt he was going to like very much. He didn't have to look at people whom he despised every day, like in Belize City.

Chetumal was so much nicer than Belize City—different as night and day, except for the weather and the city being on the Caribbean shores, or sort of as it sat on the Chetumal Bay, with the Caribbean about twenty miles to the east past the bay and the peninsula culminating southward to the island of Ambergris Caye of Belize. There was no trash in the streets, and most, if not all, of the avenues had medians lined with green, lush grass, palm trees, and other assorted ones. Most of the regular streets did not. There were no iron-barred shops keeping employees out of reach from their customers. There were no stray dogs going about the streets, defecating and fornicating all around. There were no homeless people sprawled out under the shaded canopies and begging for money. There weren't the common kinds of thievery and murderous activity so frequently occurring in Belize City.

There were street or avenue signs so that you knew where the hell you were. Not in Belize City. If you didn't know where you were, then good luck with that. The egg yolks didn't disintegrate in a chaotic dispersion when you cracked the egg. The bananas were firm and fresh, unlike in Belize where they turned to mush within a day. Precious few businesses had air-conditioning in Belize City; many did in Chetumal. An eight-ounce can of Coca-Cola cost five pesos, or about a quarter, in Chetumal. You couldn't get an eight-ounce can of Coca-Cola in Belize City.

John figured there were two universal beverages in the world other than water and milk, and those would be coffee and Coca-Cola. He loved them both.

Three liters of orange juice was thirty-five pesos, or about two dollars, in Chetumal. John could cook two scrambled eggs, three strips of bacon, grilled scalloped potatoes, and a slice of grilled bread for about fifty US cents.

"Why were these neighbors so markedly different?" John wondered. The Mexicans are a largely industrious people. The Belizeans, not so much. He could now put Molly's water bowl in the freezer; in Belize, she had to wait until night when John brought his beer and bag of ice to drink cold water. Molly didn't know where she was, but she knew the

water was colder, and she had twice the space to roam in, both inside and out. And Mexico was on Eastern Standard Time, thus in sync with the States whereas Belize was not. Why, he didn't know. In fact, because of the large tourism source from the east coast of the States, Quintana Roo chose a couple of years before to mirror that of the eastern time zone of the States. Most of the people in Chetumal were very friendly and tried to help you in any kind of way they could, although very few spoke any English. In Belize City, most were sizing you up for what they could get from you. John didn't feel like a foreigner; he felt welcomed with open arms, so unlike Belize City. If he were to find and marry a woman, the right woman, he might stay there for good.

John had whisked himself away from the monotonous hell of King's Park in Belize City. He and Molly were seemingly confined to their shoebox of a living quarter due to the heat, and he had no friends other than George next door and Carlos, Nelly's son. But Carlos was terribly immature for a twenty-four-year-old young man, and he was prone to dishonesty and thievery—that would never change. He hated Nelly now and loathed her common-law husband, Ray. He also disliked Frank, the owner, who had treated John unfairly during his last year there. John felt numb with emptiness in a dark, entropic, and desperate world over which he seemingly had no control.

"I'm so tired of being tired, sure as night will follow day. Some things I worry about never happen anyway. I keep crawling back to you. Hey, baby, there's something in your eyes, trying to say to me, everything's going to be all right. But I believe in you, it's all I want to do."

But there was no "you"—only his loyal dog and companion of fourteen years, Molly.

John had blown out a flip-flop a week before at the Plaza de la Americas on Insurgentes Avenue, the main passageway from west to east and vice versa on the north side of the city, a few kilometers to the northwest. John had gone there with Olga, her daughter, Maya, and her husband, Ricardo. In the food court at the mall, there was McDonald's, Domino's Pizza, and an Americano-Cajun-style restaurant. Further east on Insurgentes, there was a Home Depot, and still farther down, toward the eastern side of the bay, was a Walmart.

John almost felt like he was back home in the States. It was just so much cheaper there. John wondered how that could be, especially for imported American grocery products like Coca-Cola and Kellogg's cereal, and toiletry items—many, many of the things one might find at Walmart in Chetumal. They cost less than half of what they cost back in the States. John was still on the fence on that one, but he decided to chalk it up to each of the country's general cost and standard of living. In a word or two, each country's respective wealth. *But that same paradigm didn't apply to Belize,* reflected John. *I guess I simply don't understand it.*

He had taken his blown-out flip-flop to a *zapato* repair shop to the east on San Salvador and picked them up that day. Most of the buildings on the avenue were of stone masonry shielding the cinder blocks from within and, unlike in Belize, well-kept and in nonvibrant colors, mostly white, beige, and yellow for the most part. Stands of tacos and burritos vendors lined the south side of the avenue. The other businesses were largely nail and beauty salons, doctor and dental offices, and clothing stores, all of which were for *mujeres.* And there were Volkswagen beetles all over the streets from the late sixties and early seventies, probably bought secondhand from their original owners in the States. Those amazing little cars were now about a half-century old and still chugging along in the streets of Chetumal.

Taxis were the main mode of transportation for the people of Chetumal. They were everywhere—little white cars with a yellow stripe down the side at the level of the rear-view mirror. Fares were simple and, therefore, not subject to scrutiny. Go anywhere in the city, and it was twenty pesos or about a dollar. The avenues in John's area running north and south had the names of Italian cities. On his adjacent corner ran Palermo Street, and farther east were Sicilia, Napoles, and Florencia. John didn't know the connection between Chetumal and Italy, if there ever was one.

John had called Olga from Belize City about a month before to inquire about lodging for two weeks for him and Molly. His interest was simply to reset his visa so that the onerous one-hundred-dollar-per-month nonresident ex-patriot fee would be reduced to fifty dollars per month for a six-month period. He then had planned to move to a place supposedly known as Twin Cayes, where an old lady he had met in May, courtesy of his then-neighbor, George, had told him she owned ten acres of land just east of Dangriga toward the sea and allegedly had fifteen cabanas, replete with private baths and flat-screen televisions. She, Mirna, a petite and relatively fit woman in her early eighties and of Garifuna lineage, said that she was getting too old to run the place, such as sometimes having to cook for forty or fifty people at a time and having to maintain the dozen or so kayaks that guests used for navigating the tributaries running parallel to the sea. She told John that she wanted him to come and live there and run the place, and she would deed to him half of the property. John thought that she was probably once, long ago, a pretty lady.

She would then tell John that he was shy and touch him while they sat and talked on her bed in George's room. She would stroke him on his back or arms. "Please come, okay? I charge only one hundred dollars per week. And you'll love it. I'll grill you fish, like red snapper and mahi-mahi, and we can drink beer together. It will be wonderful," Mirna would say to John, almost every day of that strange weeklong visit to George's room at the guesthouse.

None of this makes any sense to me, John thought. *She allegedly owns this wonderful resort of sorts, but she's here in Belize City with her daughter, both with no money, and staying in George's room. It's insane, they're both insane*, John concluded.

Mirna kept telling John of this utopia, of this paradise, and it could all be his or, well, half of it could be his.

And, John thought to himself, *we're going to ride horses bareback on the beach at sunset, and we'll both be topless and gazing into each other's eyes, all the while smiling with that smitten look on each of our faces. I'll be like Vladimir Putin—although, I really think he's gay—and you, Mirna, my dear, I don't really know who you would look like because it would be an unprecedented moment in the annals of absurdity. Well, anyway, we'll frolic in the sun-splashed foam of the surf and gaze out into the aqua clear waters of the Caribbean. Oh, this must be heaven, it must be but a dream. Then we'll roast mahi-mahi over an open-pit bonfire and throw in some potatoes and asparagus to boot, still gazing in adoration and amazement into one another's eyes, and then . . . I'll run as fast as I can to my cabana and lock the door.*

John would then laugh to himself. *This is good stuff,* John thought. *You can't make it up.*

John dubbed her *Malady Mirna,* and so it was to be. *And she still has hormones for sex? Is that possible? I certainly don't want to find out,* John wondered.

"How do you advertise to your North American and European guests, Mirna?" John asked her on one of those days of mental hysteria. "Is there a website for the place?"

"Yes, sure, of course there is, John."

"Well, I'd love to see it. What's the website address?"

"I don't know, somebody else does that."

She was, according to George, eighty-four years old but looked to be in her early seventies.

What a bonus, John mused.

George told John that she wanted to be his girlfriend. Unbelievable and sad but true.

She would wander off sometimes in the middle of the day or early evening, and George would have to go find her; she would sometimes be all the way downtown just standing in front of a pharmacy, maybe waiting for the next possible suitor for an encounter yet unfathomable and, hopefully, unlikely. This would be three-to-four-kilometer excursions, quite impressive for an eighty-something-year-old woman. They stayed in George's room, which was next to John's room at the Bay View Guesthouse. Her daughter was there too; a twenty-something wicked witch of a woman. She loathed Molly and hit her with a shoe once. John told her to never touch Molly again. Stalking her prey, she pounced on the weakest of the male herd—on the perimeter of their lines. Those who had strayed from the protection of their own. That stray would be George.

George came to the guesthouse in early December from Wyoming. He was about five feet and eleven inches and weighed probably two hundred plus some odd—*odd* being the operative word—pounds with a massive beer belly but never seemed to drink that much beer. He said he was sixty-four years old, and he looked every bit of it. He was originally from Mississippi and was obsessively intrigued by the Civil War. He had sandy blonde hair, which was short all around but with a mullet, and blue eyes. His hair was becoming sun-bleached, just like John's had. Straight out the late eighties and stopped stone-cold in time. His working life had been consumed at the behest of the notoriously-infamous energy company of Houston-domicile known as Enron. He had been very kind to John, giving him much-needed medical supplies and the like, which we will get into later.

George had a propensity to go out on the streets and talk to anyone and everyone and bring home the stray felines, usually of the black persuasion. This particular duo took the cake.

It was a daughter-mother duo who could only have been dredged up by George. Where he found them, God only knows. They stayed in his room, a dual bedroom only slightly bigger than John's, for a full week—George and the witch in one bed and Mirna, the crazy old lady and mother, in the next.

Finally, and a week later, Malady Mirna and the witch of a daughter left with a two-hundred-dollar donation and bus tickets to Dangriga in hand, which George said was the least he could do in the name and presence of the Lord Jesus Christ. Whether he had ever actually had sex with the witch or not, each being equally unlikely from John's perspective, would remain a mystery to John. And in the presence of the old lady, asleep or not? A mystery John didn't want to know the answer to.

The following morning, John fixed breakfast in his own kitchen for the first time in over two-and-a-half years. Scrambled *huevos* and *tocino*; it was wonderful. John couldn't remember if he had had any bacon in Belize. He went down to the street beside the narrow walkway leading back to the entry gate to the concrete courtyard.

Through the gate and ten paces to the street and left, John went to the Super Aki and bought a pillow, a bowl, a knife, seasoning salt, tea, and two Coca-Colas. The grocery was not unlike those found in the States, with many more selections at about half the cost as in Belize. John liked to go to the grocery because it was air-conditioned, and he could practice his *Español*.

"*Donde esta la azukar? La frutas? La tocino? La carne? La leche?*" John would ask them all whether he wanted them or not. It was great fun, but they never seemed to understand him. One day, John asked a young woman who worked there where the tortillas were, to what she responded, "We no have." Of course, John knew where the cervezas were, and there were many to choose from and they were all good. They cost less than half of what they did in Belize. And oddly, John rarely saw Dos Equis in the stores. He guessed that the "most interesting man in the world" wasn't so interesting in Mexico. On his short walk back, he stopped in to see Carla, who was happy to see him. John asked her if she would trim a little more off the top, to which she gladly accommodated. He gave her ten pesos.

"See you soon, bye!" John said as he traversed the busy crossing to the median of San Salvador Avenue. "I hope so!" she yelled after him as John crossed San Salvador to the grass and tree-lined median separating the two sides of the avenue. Carla was an attractive young lady with medium-length brown hair, brown eyes, and of medium height with a nice body that she kept somewhat concealed, and she was probably in her early thirties. She would probably be in John's bed soon.

Later that morning, John took the *colectivo*, or van, from its stop in front of the Super Aki to the market in the city center just west of Heroes Avenue, the main shopping area running south to the Chetumal Bay. The distance from John's apartment was about three kilometers. The ride cost five pesos each way, or about a quarter. John was in search of a new phone service as his Belize service was now obsolete and unavailable. He found a Telcel store, which he priced to then discuss with Olga as to its suitability.

On the ride back to the Super Aki, John struck up a conversation with a beautiful young Mexican girl named Danella. She was very nice and spoke some English and had nice, well-appointed breasts—way up, firm, and high, not too big, not too small but just right—and long legs and a slender waist. She was in her early twenties, John figured. The older lady sitting between the two of them pointed at John and motioned with her hand to her eyes to John to indicate she had seen him before at the grocery. She was wearing the red shirt that all the employees wore. Daniella pointed at John's hair and eyes, seemingly saying that he stuck out like a sore thumb that's why the older lady had recognized him.

Before John could ask her for her number, which he quickly concluded would be too awkward at this juncture of having known her, John's stop came, and they said goodbye, hopefully to meet on the van again someday. John would soon realize that, although there were many beautiful girls in Chetumal, actually being with one would be difficult because of the language barrier.

Nonetheless, John was liking his new home and life there on San Salvador Avenue very much. John was sure he would meet a girl and fall in love yet one more time—a thought that a mere month before had seemed impossible. Ironically, on one of John's first few days in his new life, he and Olga went to the Plaza de la Americas where she went inside to the bank while John and Molly waited outside under the shaded canopy of a tree in one of the nearby grass medians. When Olga returned and they got into her mini-van, Olga told John that when she saw him sitting under that tree, she was sure he would marry again and would have many, many women to choose from.

"Take your time and don't be in such a rush. Be choosy," she said. "Be sure that the woman has values and was or is in a home with a good father. That's very important. I suspect you will want a girl in her twenties or thirties, si? There are many beautiful women in Chetumal that would love to have a handsome, intelligent American man like you. But you need to learn to speak Spanish. I'll teach you."

John had three months to "live" before his sixtieth birthday, and he intended to make the most of it. Those would be the days he would forever remember.

When John returned home that early afternoon, he saw Carla across the street in her open-air Estetica Carla parlor giving a pedicure to a woman. He crossed the median when she had motioned for John to come over, and he asked her for an envelope so that he could write to Alan and Abby, his youngest children back in Atlanta, to tell them that he had moved to Mexico. Alan had stopped writing to John in early January, and he hadn't communicated with Abby at all in well over a year. John thanked Carla for the envelope, and it was then that he realized it probably wouldn't be a good idea for her to be in his bed after all, although she was kind and sweet.

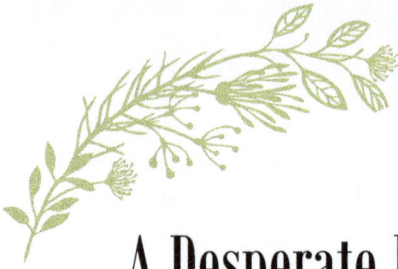

A Desperate Escape from Belize

John was desperate to get out of the Bay View Guesthouse and never to return. He found a hostel on the internet that he thought he had stayed on his journey to Belize City two and a half years before. Luckily, he now had a cell phone, which he could use to make yet another desperate escape.

"I would like to stay for two weeks in your inn with myself and my dog, her name's Molly. I believe we stayed there for one night between Christmas and the New Year about two and a half years ago," John said.

"Maybe, but I don't think so, but sure, you can come and stay with your dog," Olga responded.

Olga Cervantes Lopez was the proprietor of the Posada Inn on Venustiano Carranza Avenue, just one block south of John's new apartment. Olga was Mexican, originally from Monterrey, who had lived for twenty or so years in Haiti where she was married. She was an intelligent woman in her middle years and had a beautiful half-African daughter who lived around the corner named Maya. Olga's hair was jet black, and she was of medium build and height with a wonderful laugh. John and Olga would become good friends.

It was the afternoon of June 15, and John took Molly to the veterinarian in Belize City, a few miles out on the Northern Highway (cleverly named because it traversed the northern part of the country out of Belize City) to get her requisite visa to enter Mexico. She got a clean bill of health, although the veterinarian said that she had cataracts in each eye, and he suspected she had a heart irregularity, neither of which were uncommon in a dog of her age, which was now fourteen. While waiting for the physician, a lady approached John and Molly and said, "Remember me, I'm the one who took care of Molly while you were away?"

"Yes, I remember, but it was so long ago, a year now," John responded. "Do you work here?"

Terchie said, "No, I'm here applying to be the dog groomer for the store."

"Really? What a coincidence that we would meet here like this."

"Isn't it so, right?" she said.

She petted Molly as Molly did, indeed, remember her, but she was happy to go on her way with her visa in staid order, and with her master, probably remotely aware of an impending journey. John could tell when Molly knew someone from the past and if and when she was comfortable being around a person other than himself.

John and Molly were ready to set sail in the morning to get away from a dreadful situation, a dreadful city, and a dreadful country.

They caught the eleven-thirty bus to the border and were on the way, finally, out of Belize. The bus trudged along slowly to the northwest to Orange Walk, stopping many, many times for entering and exiting passengers. From Orange Walk, they headed to the northeast for Corozal, which was on the coast and lay just to the southwest of Chetumal on the bay, as Molly sat quietly and patiently in her mobile cage at the back of the bus. Mexicana and reggae music accompanied their satisfying journey, yet farther and farther, away from their existing hell, or at least John's.

From Corozal was a short ten-kilometer ride to the border. The ride from Belize City to Chetumal was about sixty kilometers or a hundred miles. They departed the bus at about four o'clock and embarked upon Belize customs. A rotund black man sat at the security checkpoint and said, "Remember me, John Headley? I'm the one who brought you in at immigration in Belize City. Sorry about that. My boss made me do it. Did you finish your book?"

"Oh yeah, I remember you, and I hope I don't see you again. Yes, I finished my book, and you're in it. How are you, and what are you doing here?" John said with a sheepish grin.

"Rotations, you know. They sent me up here."

They exchanged pleasantries, and as John picked up Molly and the rest of his belongings, he said—and meant it—"Good to see you, take good care now." And John was on his way to a new life.

Olga's inn sat on the north side of the street, and she was sitting in the open-air foyer as John and Molly got out of the cab. It was a three-story building of white masonry with a red roof. There was a gate to the inn into the converted garage of tile flooring where there were several large cushioned chairs, a book case, a circular glass-top table with four chairs, and ancient Mystica and African art all around. Long, scared faces of long ago gazed down from the walls as one got the sense of the many people who had lived there on the coast many, many centuries before. Poised in the center back of the entry room was a painting, which stood on an easel, of a snowcapped volcano in central Mexico with a beautiful white castle with two yellow domes and a turret as well in the foreground and in the lush green valley below awash with sunflowers. John would later learn that Olga had painted it herself.

A large living area sat through the large wooden door entering the inn, which was once a private residence. Olga's computer and credenza was straight on the front left of the room, and a large sofa and dining table led to the kitchen. Up the first flight of stairs, the stairs branched to the left and right to the seven or so rooms upstairs along with six bathrooms—five being private—and the male and female dorm rooms were side by side in the front right of the hostel. The men's dorm was on the front side of the house overlooking the street below. It housed five bunk beds with a large sliding glass window facing south to the bay, which was some two kilometers away, where the ocean winds provided some relief during the day and was most comfortable in the evening and night. The walls were painted a gentle hue of green and more Mystica pieces of art were on the walls throughout the second level.

John stayed in the men's dorm as it was the cheapest at about 175 pesos a day. They had the room to themselves all but one of his and Molly's fifteen-day stay there, when a young blonde male from Manchester was passing through on his way to Cancun for his flight home. John and Molly sat out on the veranda every night while John enjoyed his *cervezas* or *vino*. It was June 18, a Saturday, when John had his first glass of wine in about two and a half years. That day marked the one-year anniversary of his arrest in Belize. It was cause for celebration.

That night is when John told Olga of his stay in prison and the rest of the hellish twelve months that had followed his prison stint there in Belize the year before.

"You were what? You were thrown in prison? For doing what?" Olga asked.

"My visa had expired for essentially the entire time I had been there. In Belize, unlike Mexico or most any other country I suppose, you have to report to immigration monthly and pay a hundred-dollar fee to continue legally staying as a nonresident resident. It's a long story, but I'll tell you the highlights, or lowlights, as it were," John responded.

John told her about the arrest and the setup, the "sting," leading up to it along with the first couple of weeks in prison.

"And so the Fourth of July weekend had come and gone with no sign of or word from Nelly," John told Olga. "I didn't know if or when I would get out of that prison. She could have skipped town with my bank card for all I knew. Well, finally, that following Thursday afternoon, a guard came to the cell and said, 'John Headley, pack it up. Let's go, c'mon, hurry. Immigration is waiting for you up front.'"

"I was just so relieved and excited to be getting out of prison with all those strange, scary men, but I knew something had gone wrong with my bank account," John told Olga.

The same guy named Robert, who had driven John to the prison three long weeks ago, was there waiting at the processing and administrative office at the entrance of the prison and, after collecting his belongings and changing out of the orange jump-suit, off they went, headed back to immigration in Belize City. After checking in at the office, Robert was kind enough, although otherwise wouldn't have been allowed, to drive John back to the guesthouse. John didn't have a penny on him.

Nelly was there as it turned evening in Belize, but Molly wasn't as she was at the lady's house who had been so kind to take her in.

"Nelly told John that she had been thrown in jail over suspicion of how she had received her car, which was very nice by Belizean standards and couldn't have possibly been paid for by her own legitimate money. Turns out, some man from Canada had bought the car and had it put into her name. It was obviously bought with laundered money. Well, it turns out, according to Nelly anyway, that the man was in prison in Mexico for some sort of scam. She told me that the police demanded five hundred dollars to release her, and she had used my card to get the money. Ain't that screwed up?" John said to Olga.

"Well, that's not very nice. She shouldn't have done that, that's for sure," Olga said.

"No shit," John responded.

Nelly gave back to John his card, and he walked down to the Princess Hotel and Casino and saw that he only had three hundred and eighty-five dollars in his account, which had to last him until the next month, that being August.

All his things had been packed up from his room and moved to one of the opposite side, downstairs rooms with ugly wooden floors and no private bath. Frank had done this to John, and he also discovered that it was Carlos who had packed his things and stolen fifty dollars, some beeswax, and a nice bottle opener. "Frank said I had no proof of such things being stolen. Fuck Frank," was John's conclusion.

Later that night, the kind lady named Terchie, who had taken care of Molly during those long and painful three weeks of John being in prison, brought Molly to the guesthouse. It was a happy and emotional reunion. Molly cried in high-pitched yelps as she often did when she was reunited with her master. The scars on both of her sides from the dog attack were still visible. It was the ninth of July, as it is as of this writing, only one year later.

Terchie was a remnant of the long-since departed Humane Society there in Belize City. There was little humane about Belize City.

Molly now slept about twenty hours a day, and she was losing her hearing and probably her eyesight too. But she was happy and comfortable, and that's all that mattered to John. John had never, and probably would never again, feel such love for and from an animal.

On the twentieth of July of 2015, John was in a desperate need of money. It was a Monday morning, and he would never forget the agony and uncertainty he felt that morning. He had two options to pursue in hopes of getting any money to last him for the next eleven days. John knew that immigration had miscalculated his arrearages for his passport violation. As he calculated, they had charged through September, not July as they should have done. He figured they owed him one hundred dollars. He also had his laptop that he hoped that he could pawn at a pawnshop directly on the way to the immigration office, what was about three miles away, across the river on the Western Highway, and then on a street running parallel to the river heading northwest out of downtown. As he left the guesthouse and passed through the gate onto Baymen Avenue headed south toward town at around nine o'clock, he kept repeating to himself, "You've got to do this, you have no choice." He was off on a six-mile round-trip walk in his flip-flops, possessing no guarantees for success, in the scorching hot sun of that bleak summer morning.

The pawnshop was on the corner at the roundabout just across the bridge, which traversed the Belize River, and what corner led to immigration. John was already well covered in sweat as he waited for the pawnshop operator to show some interest in his potential collateral. He placed his laptop into a bin for the shop operator to inspect, who sat behind a glass window for security purposes.

"I'd like to pawn the computer until I get paid on the first of the month," John said.

The man turned on his computer and looked at the software on it. After a couple of minutes of inspecting it, he said, "I'll loan you eighty dollars,"

"Okay," John said with a big sigh of relief.

With eighty dollars in his pocket, John left the shop headed for the office of immigration, an entity that he had no loss of love or gratitude for. A small black boy came up to him on his way and said, "Sir, can you give me dollar?"

"No, go see your mother," John snapped back at him. He wiped his brow in the steamy hot sun and trudged along further.

John hated to be that way but hated even worse the situation that he was in.

Goddamn, Nelly! The nerve and gall for her to put me in this situation is unbelievable, John thought as his loathing of her was at a boiling point. It reminded him of the hatred he had felt for his second wife as they were going through their divorce.

A young Latino girl, probably in her late teens or early twenties, approached John from a side street on the river side of the street. "Hi, would you like to come back with me back to my place and have a little fun?" she said. She was pretty, and she was sexy in her halter top and blue jean shorts.

"No thanks, I've got some business to tend to," John said. *Her parents were probably at work*, John thought as he pressed along ever closer to the beige four-story office building on the right. He had about a half-mile to go.

John hadn't been there since his incarceration about a month earlier. He walked into the immigration office through the double-wooden doors to the left and saw behind the clerks' windows the two holding rooms that he and those young girls from El Salvador had been held in.

John gave the clerk his passport and said, "I think you miscalculated this payment I made for my passport." After a minute or two of research and calculating the simple math, she said, "Yes, you're right."

"Okay, good," John said. She stepped away and stood with who was presumably her supervisor, and then came back to the window and said to John, "We've updated your records and you are paid through to September 26."

"I don't want the credit for the money, I want to leave this country. I want my money back," John said to the fat black woman.

"We can't do that, it's already in the system."

"Then change the system."

"We can't do that, sir," she said, holding firm as other employees began to watch, wondering if John would explode. All of them were women and were black, except for Richard, the young Hispanic man that had driven John both to and from the prison, who stood watching in the background, not claiming any affiliation with the enraged American man.

"Goddamn it, your country is fucked up. And that's because you're all poor and stupid," John said to her as he stormed out of the office and back out into the inferno for the second leg of his six-mile journey.

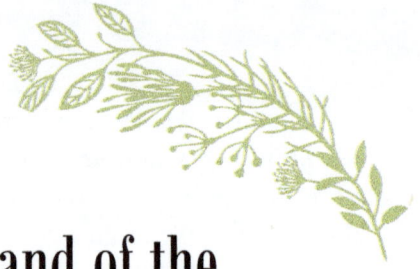

Episodes with and of the Female Persuasion

T hat Saturday night, being John's first weekend in his new apartment and one year later, John went to a gentlemen's club that the bus driver out of Mexico from the border to Corozal the week before had told John about in downtown Chetumal, where the women were fine. The club was named Aracifus, which in Spanish means "coral reef." The reef, known as the Great Aracifus, was not far off the coast and spans from and between Cozumel and Playa del Carmen, about two hundred and fifty miles to the south around the cays off the coast of central Belize. It is the second largest reef in the world, second only to the Great Barrier Reef off the coast of Australia. John and Maria had gone snorkeling around and above the massive reef some sixteen years before, on what was mainly a rum-drinking party with loud, but good, music playing that happened to be on a boat along with other guests from the all-inclusive resort in Cozumel. John remembered one of the boat's mates pointing out Sylvester Stallone's home off to the left on the island as they headed south toward their reef-snorkeling rendezvous.

John went there on a premonition that he would be approached by the most beautiful girl in the club and seduced for an impending rendezvous. After ordering a Modelo, not five minutes passed when John was tapped on the back of his right shoulder by a girl. He turned and she said, "Hi, what is your name? I can tell that you are bad boy," she said.

"Headley, John Headley," John responded.

She said "Oh, I like."

"What is your name?" John asked.

"Margareth," she said.

"I'm not a bad boy but a good boy."

She laughed and said, "We drink together?"

"Sure," John said as the attendant ushered them to a private couch against the wall on the right side of the club. John didn't notice the near-naked women dancing on stage, twirling around those shiny, bright poles.

"Where are you from?" she asked John.

"Atlanta, and you?"

"Oh my, Atlanta! Americano, si? I thought so."

"Si."

"Guadalajara," she responded.

"You're a long way from home," John said.

She now wore only a bra and panties with high heels, and she was exquisite.

"You're the most *hermosa chica* in this place," John said.

"And you're the most *guapo* man *aqui*. I love your eyes, they're so *azul*," she said.

Her breasts were firm and enticing and her legs were long and firm, all sculpted by the Goddess of Mujeres. She had a small tattoo above her breasts, which was the name of her only daughter. What the name was, John couldn't remember. Her hair was hazel, long, and straight, and her eyes were the color of caramel. She had an ornament in her belly button, and she was so fine. She looked to be more American than Mexican, not that one looks better than the other. John felt like an unconstrained eight-year-old child in a candy store, deciding what delectable object to touch first.

We'll fly away, just you and me, and make love atop the highest cloud. Our bodies will have boundless thirst and stamina for the other's pleasure, John thought to himself as they gazed into each other's eyes.

"How old are you?" she asked. Her English was better than John's Spanish, which was nil.

"You guess," John replied and then asked, "How old are you? Let me guess . . . twenty-four."

"Si, exactly," she said. "You're forty-five, I think."

"Close, I'm forty-nine. *Gracias* for the compliment," John said. *A white lie it was, no, it wasn't white but rather one in bold crimson,* John thought to himself but necessary at that stage of the game.

"*Quisiera tu,*" John said to Margereth.

"I no work manana. Let's see each other tomorrow night," she said.

"Okay, I'd very much like that," John said.

They were very much attracted to one another, touching each other's face and hair. John gave her directions to come the following evening to his apartment. She wrote her name on the back of Olga's business card, phone number, and e-mail address.

"Take a taxi and tell him to take you to the corner of the Super Aki on San Salvador Avenue at eight, okay?" John said.

"Yes, the corner of the Super Aki on San Salvador Avenue, *ocho en punto,*" she repeated.

All the while, she had her arms firmly around his shoulders and neck on the couch while in her scant laced panties and revealing bra. She softly and sweetly kissed John's lips. John wanted to make love to her right there on the couch but quickly concluded that it wouldn't be appropriate.

"Oh no, we have a problem," John said to Margaret.

"I know," she said as she caressingly placed her hand on his crotch and gently stroked the much-aroused and now muscular organ.

"You'll have to excuse him, *por favor,* he has a mind of his own," John said.

She laughed as she slowly withdrew her hand, knowing that it would raise, among other things, attention. But she didn't want to stop. It's a wonderful thing when a beautiful woman desires something sexual with you. It is a powerful thing, this thing we call lust. She wanted to see and feel the gushing of the volcanic-like eruption of lust streaming down her fingers and then later drink it from the same, well, not so much, fountain of youth.

"He will rest well tomorrow night after some tender loving care," she said.

She had to go. It was her time to dance. "See you tomorrow night," she said before heading for the stage.

"Please be there," John said.

"I will be there," she said as they crossed pinkies in a vow of sorts. John left as she began her performance. He didn't want to watch.

When John got home, he went over with his laptop to Estetica Clara's to go on line. She was happy to see him. John showed her pictures of his children and ex-wife and pictures of his homes in Connecticut and Atlanta as they sat around a small table at the front of the shop facing the sidewalk and the avenue beyond. She was stunned by their largess and their beauty. "One would never find such homes in Belize," she said. He told her about his book, which was about to be published, and she said to John, "You're famous, like Ricky Iglasias."

The first girl John had taken to his apartment was a twenty-seven-year-old Mexican who was staying at the Posada Inn on her way to Mexico City the following afternoon. John met her the night before the gentlemen's club, tryst. John went over to Olga's in the evening for their planned thrice-weekly English-Spanish lessons at six o'clock. John introduced himself, and she told him her name was Nakhida. She was pretty, not beautiful, but nonetheless pretty, and had a great body. She had ridden her bicycle from Merida through Cancun and Playa del Carmen, on to Tulum and Bacalar and into Chetumal for the flight to Mexico City. She had ridden her bicycle an astonishing 380 kilometers. As one might imagine, her legs were ripped.

"Do you like *cerveza*?" John asked.

"No, not really," Nakhida said.

"How 'bout *vino*?"

"Yes, *me gusta*," she replied.

"Would you like to come with me to mi apartment for some vino later on, say, *nueve*?"

"Okay, sure," she replied.

"Great, I'll be here at nine."

John picked her up—on foot, of course—at nine, and they walked back to his apartment. John showed her some pictures of his children and ex-wife as they shared a bottle of Shiraz.

"Do you have any children?" John asked.

"No," she said.

"Have you ever been married?"

"No, and never will be," she responded.

"Why is that?"

"Because I like girls," she replied. "I'm a lesbian."

"Really?" John managed to stammer out of his mouth, clearly taken aback by the revelation.

"Si, really," she said.

"Wow, that's a shame. What a waste," John clumsily responded. Nakhida awkwardly laughed.

"You've never . . . with a man?"

"No, never," she replied.

"Really, how unusual."

"What do you do, use your tongue?"

"Si, and fingers."

"Mmm . . . I see, yeah . . . right . . ." John couldn't help but think of Austin Powers in the movie, *The Spy Who Shagged Me*.

"It must be hard being in such a minority, although I'm not saying there's anything wrong with it," John even more clumsily said.

"Oh, I don't think it's such a minority," she responded.

"It can last four or five hours with many orgasms. Can men do that? No, I think not."

"How do you know?" John asked.

"Many partners have told me. Some like it both ways, not me. Ooh . . . yuck, a man? No, not me."

John was stunned and aghast. This had never happened to him in his near sixty years—well, the near forty-five years of operative relevance. The first fifteen didn't count.

I wonder if the growing prevalence of gay and lesbian people could be Mother Nature's way of reacting to an increasingly untenable growth in population? Hmmm . . . Nietsche-like, I know, but food for thought, John later thought.

"Hey, you sociology professors at Harvard and Yale and all your other smug institutions collectively known as the Ivy League. Do some research. Gather some empirical data, not normative stuff like I'm spouting. We, as accountants, pontificate that assets equal liabilities plus stakeholder equity, but there might be some other things lurking in between. It's worth taking a look at. I bet the lesbian rate is currently about 2.5 out of every 100 women. And I bet that a hundred years ago, the rate was less than half that. What is the correlative, or causal effect, of this phenomenon? It's that there's too many goddamn people on this planet, that's what it is. Trust me, I know what I'm talking about on this one."

That was pretty much the end of that night. *Cest le vie*, John thought as he walked Nakhida back to the inn. *Adios, amiga. Hasta luego.* Don't let the door hit you from behind. No, really, she was a nice girl, just from a different world.

John continued his conversation with Nakhida as he walked back to his apartment.

"So let's play out a hypothetical. Let's say, you are the only woman left on this planet, and there's only one guy, we'll call him Adam. It's just the two of you anywhere to be found. You both happen to live in the same neighborhood. Would you have sex with Adam for the sake of all humanity and its future? Or would you say, 'Adam? Ooh, yuck. I'd rather use my fingers,'" John asked her.

"Ah, that's what I thought," John said. "Go ahead, try it. You might like it."

Back in Belize, John was growing more and more impatient with Nelly. He began to hate the sight of her; she seemed to think nothing of the wrong that she had perpetrated on John. She never made eye contact with John. John was sure it was a defense mechanism, albeit innate, whereby the offender turns the table on his or her victim, making them to blame, forever seeking out their perceived flawed traits and then telling themselves. "See, I told you so, he's such a jerk."

And then there was Frank, the Taiwanese man who seemed to have no friends and avoided the guests also. *Have you ever noticed that most Asian men have no personality?* John thought. That phenomenon goes all the way back to John's sophomore year at the University of Tennessee when Mark and John's suite mate was a twenty-something-year-old from South Korea working on his doctorate in physics. He stayed holed up in his room solving equations on computer printout paper with his pen until all hours of the night while eating kimchi, that nasty, spicy hot cabbage they so adored. He was a barrel of laughs all right. A rigorous and seasoned party-animal like John and Mark, he was not.

The mother of Frank's young daughter, a beautiful yellow Creole woman in her late twenties or early thirties, had moved out over a year before, and Frank just stayed holed up in his bunker upstairs in the older building. John knew that he had overcharged him for his room both upstairs and downstairs in the hellhole on the back side right. It amounted to about $1,500. And now he wouldn't even let John and Molly go back to his preferred room upstairs with the large private balcony looking out over the park and the sea.

The next week and a half until the end of July was pure hell. Nelly told John she couldn't pay him back until she sold the car, and it was in the shop for engine repairs of origin unknown to John. By the twentieth of the month, John had run out of money. He had to rely on Nelly to fix him any food that he might have, a woman he now hated. She never once said anything more about using his card; no apology, no nothing.

During the day, the room became so hot, it was unbearable. The floor fan was old and weak. There was a Hispanic young couple with a young son in the room by the bath and then Nelly, Ray, and their personality-less son, Ryan, on the other side. Someone was seemingly always in the bathroom. John would get up before everyone else and shower around six o'clock. If it weren't for the television, John surely would have lost his mind, but at least, he thought, he wasn't in prison and he had Molly.

August came and went with no sign of Nelly selling her car or John being able to move back to his old room upstairs. She wouldn't even put her phone number on the back—a common practice in Belize as virtually anything and everything was for sale—for fear that it would draw more attention from the police. Nelly told John that Frank didn't want Molly upstairs anymore. Asshole. Frank avoided John; he was afraid of him.

In mid-September, John was able to move back to the other side, but only this time not his beloved room but one on the first floor, along with two other rooms which surrounded the kitchen.

And back in Chetumal, the day after the tryst with Margareth, John stopped into the western-most *farmacia* on his block, which was on the corner across the street from the Super Aki. He asked one of the clerks behind the counter for a public phone card, as he wanted to call Margereth, as she had no way of contacting him. He couldn't get into his Yahoo! e-mail or a new Gmail account that Jorge, a very nice high school kid who didn't speak any English and Olga's weekend worker, set up for him the day before. Somehow that account said that the password didn't match the address too. He said in Spanish that he didn't understand and a young *bonita chica* at the other end of the counter looked up from what she was doing and smiled at John and pointed to her eyes, as if to say, "You're eyes."

It happened in Belize, and now it was happening here, John thought to himself as he approached the non-English speaking *chica* with bright, beaming eyes and smile.

"*Donde esta la publica telefonos?*" John asked as she just kept smiling at him in a sheepish, playful manner. He pointed across the parking lot and she kept smiling. "*Hasta luego*," John said as he left and she giggled and smiled and repeated the same.

It seemed to John that girls in their twenties and even teens were infatuated with him, but if they were in their forties and fifties, they paid him no attention. Women in their thirties were in the crossover zone; some yes, some no. *One of life's little mysteries, I guess*, John thought, although he supposed it could be worse, as in the reverse.

Women are to men as cats are to dogs. Woman stalk their prey cunningly and discreetly, men—with their guns a blazing—front and headlong. Women are patient and unassuming in their quests; men dive into their target before it is ready. Men go straight to the issue at hand; women are content to leave it for another day. There is a time and place for everything; men simply don't know either.

When it came to women, John couldn't remember how many times he had heard his friends say to him, "You dog, you."

"Well, somebody has to do it, it might as well be me," John would always reply.

They would laugh boastfully at the masculinity of their cama-raderie and love of the conquest. He missed his old friends, but that was another time, another place.

That evening, as the descending sun was bringing an end to John's first week as a resident of Mexico, he sat gazing out the double windows in the kitchen facing south toward the bay. The oncoming cumulous clouds, in their prevalent and endless journey from south-east toward northwest, were seemingly reaching upward—largely the effect of the curvature of the earth—like blooming mushrooms over the vast crevasse below of the sea and the depths beneath it, in and of itself a whole other world. Molly slept peacefully and contently under the fan and the constant drone it afforded, much like the comfort of the whistle and the rumblings of a far-off train in the dead of night.

"Why did you continue living there?" Olga asked, as John continued to describe his experience in Belize.

"Well, I had Molly, and unless I wanted to live on the southwest side of the river with the blacks and where the crime rate was sky-high, there weren't a lot of options," John replied. "I guess also I was a bit lazy. If it weren't for Fox News and ESPN, I believe I would have gone crazy, if I'm not already."

"You're not, trust me, you're not," Olga said.

John had become very anal among those days there at the Bay View Guesthouse. Presumably the early stages of lunacy, he reckoned. His room key and cloth for wiping his brow while walking, as well as his reading glasses, had to be in his left pocket. Dollar bills had to be in ascending order of value and folded three times. He tried to carry at least five coins so that he could shuffle them between his right thumb and index finger; these, along with his identification, all must be in his right pocket. He eschewed the two-dollar bill and would ask that it be changed for two one-dollar coins. His room had to be spotless at all times. He never left more than three cigarette butts in his tuna can ashtray. But these were not rituals of mystical superstitious hijinks; they were simply a sign of having too much time on his hands, or at least so he thought.

Time was measured in five-minute intervals. John was always waiting for the next thing to do as the long, hot days dragged on, sometimes seemingly endlessly. Sometimes when John had to go somewhere like downtown to buy cigarettes or used clothing or the immigration office or the K-Park grocery store, all in the blistering heat, he would say to himself, "You have to do this, you have to do this. You have no choice."

"Well, it's in the early morning, we really should get to bed," John said to Olga.

"Yes, but I want you to tell me the rest tomorrow, okay?"

"Si, we'll carry on with the story from hell tomorrow night. Good night, *buenos noches*," and John headed upstairs to his unoccupied dorm where Molly was already long fast asleep.

Two days after the tryst, or eight days into his new life, John went over to Carla's Estetica Carla salon to get on the internet. He could see when she was in the salon easily from his bedroom window. It was more often than not that she wouldn't be, leaving the salon unattended while doing chores in the back, where her house was. If one were to do that in Belize City, all the furniture would be gone within a day. It was more often than not in Central America for small business owners to live on the same premises as their stores and shops, either above or in back. She lived there above her salon with her father and brother, who John had yet to meet.

He showed her his new book that was coming out, and she read out loud the back cover and then looked at the front cover and said, "That is your house in Atlanta! Si?"

"Yes, was my house in Atlanta," John replied.

"And why did you sell it?"

"I didn't want to, I lost it. Seemingly all tied to a nasty divorce."

"Why? I'm so sorry."

"It's a long story, it's all in the book."

"But I want to know now."

"In due time, dear, in due time."

They listened to music on YouTube; she picked her song, then John picked his, over and over for hours. She chose some very good current Spanish performers from the Caribbean, of which John wasn't familiar, and then Adele, Beyoncé, and even Brian Adams and Conway Twitty.

They flirted innocently like kids in high school—not sure of what they felt or why they felt it—while John drank beer under the canopy of stars on San Salvador Avenue. They playfully berated one another for their different cultures and different worlds, although they both liked and respected each of which from they had come. Carla had dark, Auburn hair with eyes to match and high cheek bones reflecting some Mayan descent. Her body was toned but not easily discernable, as she was dressed in somewhat—well, not tight—white shorts and a loose button-up blouse. She never dressed provocatively, or at least as long as John had known her. Her hair was always pulled up in a tight, short ponytail while she worked (she wouldn't put in down, although John asked her to—too hot, she explained), and her smile was happy and full of life. She was thirty years of age and had no children and had never lived with a man. *What's not to like?* John asked himself, and then he quickly had an answer: *But she lives with her father and brother.* Sometimes, you take what you can get.

She pressed John—she was a persistent woman—as to why he had divorced his two wives. Actually, John hadn't divorced either; they divorced him but he didn't mention that.

"Well, the Argentinian, we just grew apart, but I really think it had to do with the death of my son, Brandon. I didn't feel like she had supported me enough through that most difficult time and I resented it, but I was still in love with her. I think the seeds had already been sewn though."

"You lost your son?"

"Yes, many years ago."

"How?

"Leukemia," John answered.

"Cancer . . . of the blood?"

"Yes, you could say that."

"I'm so sorry."

"Thank you."

"With my first wife, I had had an affair, and ultimately, I think, that caused the divorce," John said.

"You had an affair? Fuck you," responded Carla.

"Whoa, easy now," John said. "But that is exactly what I had in mind. Just kidding," John said, not being able to resist the urge. He didn't think the word *fuck* could possibly come out of her mouth. She was so prim and proper.

"I'm sorry, I didn't mean that," she said.

"It was over twenty-five years ago," John responded in a futile attempt of self-defense.

"Don't you want a girl? Don't you need a girl? Why don't you have a girl? You and no girl, come on."

"Sure, I want a girl, I need a girl. Don't you want, don't you need a man?

"Yes, I want a man, and I need a man," she said.

Good, John thought to himself. *At least she's not a lesbian. Well then, she's only thirty. I'm sure she has a strong sexual appetite that hasn't been fed for quite a while, I'm guessing.*

She said she loved American music. She sang along with her chosen songs, and John played air guitar on his. John chose, of course, the Rolling Stones's "*Almost Heard You Sigh*" as his first choice, and then on to Johnny Cash's "*Hurt*," Sting's "*Desert Rose*" and "*Fields of Gold*," Tom Petty's "*Crawling Back to You*," Chris Isaac's "*Wicked Game*," Foreigner's "*I've Been Waiting for a Girl Like You*," Coldplay's "*Paradise*" (that was in memory of you, dear daughter Abby), and ended the night, while she was falling asleep, with Pure Prairie League's "*Falling In and Out of Love with You*," and the sequel thereof, "*Aimie*."

Carla said to John, "You're falling in love with me? This is my song to sleep on, dreaming of you? The song is so pretty. I can't believe you're falling in love with me. That is so good. I'm so happy you're really falling in love with me? Don't fall out of love with me. I'm just kidding, just kidding," she said. (Her true thought, probably not)

"Good night, Carla, *buenos noches*," John said, as he shut off the laptop and turned to cross the avenue.

"*Hasta la vista*," Carla replied, and off they went to their respective worlds—she to sleep, John to write.

She's already in love with me and she's Elisa's age, John thought as he made the short walk to his apartment. *I can tell.*

John woke up before dawn the next morning thinking of Carla, a girl living in such a different world with such a different past. He wasn't even sure if he could have sex with her. In a way, she just felt like a friend to him, like Olga, but her body told John something entirely different. And he couldn't help but think of her.

"You're my blue sky, you're my sunny day. Lord, you know it makes me high when you turn your love my way, turn your love my way-ay."

But, oh, what a web we weave when we set out to deceive. The night before being with Carla, John stopped by her salon when he saw her and Edgar talking in the front entryway. Somehow, questions of age came up, and Carla was most interested in John's.

"Let me guess, you're thirty," she said to John. "Be serious. Well, that's what you look like." She giggled. "Okay, are you in your high thirties or low forties, tell me, which is it."

"It's higher," John replied.

"Really? Okay, midforties, upper forties, which is it. I want to know."

"Upper forties, that's close enough. How can you so easily go from thirty to the upper forties?" John asked.

"Tell me, forty-seven, forty-eight, forty-nine . . ."

"Bingo!"

It was vintage-like banter you would hear between a teenage girl and a targeted teenage boy in high school, hormones a-raging.

Is it possible that in my new life, I can simply reduce my age by ten years and nobody will know the difference? And it would thus be so done? Can I actually steal ten years from Mother Nature? Everybody seemed to believe it. Why not? John wondered.

Where are you going with this thing with Carla, John wondered to himself. *What about Margareth, the model and dancer. Oh yeah, well, that's a negative. Can I have them both? Maybe even at the same time? No, wake up, John, that's not you. Can I really do that? Well, maybe, why not?"*

John did his usual morning workout and made his way to the shower. He loved the new, spacious walk-in shower with no door and green tile up to about six feet and the rush of the cold water pouring over his head and body. Nobody, it seemed, in Central America showered in hot water. John remembered, in his early days in Belize, asking Nelly if her hot water was working, which was in the older building, because his wasn't. She said they didn't have hot water and never used it for bathing. She said that it didn't get you as clean.

What an idiot, John thought. *Then why do you wash your cloths in hot water?* he asked rhetorically without uttering the words. It was probably some mythical fraud perpetrated by her parents long ago when she was a child.

Anyway, the next morning, John stopped by Carla's salon on his way to the *farmacia* to buy a pack of cigarettes. "*Buenos dias*," they exchanged as he touched her right shoulder with his left hand and gave her a kiss on the cheek.

"That's what I owe you from last night," John said after he kissed her.

"Thank you, I had a very, very, very good time last night," she said.

"I'd like you to come and see my new apartment sometime today," John said.

"Okay," she said. "This afternoon when I close the salon, say, two thirty. Okay?"

"Yes," John replied. "I'll see you then."

If she shows up in that dress and with her hair down as I saw her this past Sunday when she returned from Orange Walk, I would be very happy, John thought to himself. *No, that want happen*, he quickly concluded. She opened her salon around seven-thirty in the morning, closed for siesta from about two in the afternoon until around four-thirty, and stayed open till about ten-thirty or eleven o'clock, Monday through Saturday, as was the case the night before, although no customers came during their music fest. *But then, maybe that extra thirty minutes is to get all dolled up? No, I doubt it. We'll see*, John thought, as Molly slept blissfully under the fan on her back with her legs pointing straight up into the air in the heat of the late morning.

"*I'm just waiting on a lady. I'm just waiting on a friend. Making love and breaking hearts, that is a game for you. I'm just waiting on a lady. I'm just waiting on a friend.*"

She came, but it was a different time and much later. *It's so different in that regard in Belize and Mexico than in the States. Commitments are made in such vague generalities as to be unenforceable*, John thought.

Commitments are rare in lands of the Yucatan on the western shores of the tropical Caribbean. But she did come.

She now just says, "I'll be over in a while." You take what you can get.

"You can't always get what you want. But if you try sometimes, you just might find, you get what you need."

It was three weeks before John's night spent with Carla, and he was nearing the end of his two-week stay at Olga's Posada Inn. He read a book while he was there by Stephen King called *The Dark Tower: The Gunslinger*. It was a good book but not on the level of a Hemingway or Wolfe or Steinbeck but good nonetheless. John hadn't read a book since leaving Stuart back in Florida. There were no book stores in Belize City as far as he could tell.

On John's last weekend at the Posada Inn, a girl from Argentina checked in on Friday night in wait of a flight to Puerto Vallarta. She had long blonde hair and blue eyes, and she was tall, about John's height, with a nice figure. She told John that she was of German descent, which appeared obvious to John, and her name was Katia. She was very friendly and was in college back in Buenos Aires about to graduate with a degree in hotel management.

Saturday afternoon, they sat out on the veranda and talked about what she was doing in Puerto Vallarta and what John had been doing in Belize City.

"I just returned yesterday from Belize City, it was horrible," she said.

"Why were you there?" John asked.

"One has six months to stay in Mexico, at which point, you either leave or reset your passport at an embassy in another country. I chose Belize City because Guatemala City was so far away," she said. "I flew to Mexico City and stayed one night there and then flew here before taking the bus to Belize City. You just present your passport and they stamp and you're done."

"That's good to know," John said. "I might just come back and live here."

"I would if I were you. I never want to go back to Belize City. It was so poor and the black men stare at you, it was just terrible."

She then told John about what she was doing in Mexico.

"I work as a reservationist at a hotel resort in Puerto Vallarta."

"That sounds great. I hear Puerto Vallarta is really nice. I'd love to see the sun set again into the ocean."

"Oh, yes, it's wonderful," she said, as she showed John a picture on her cell phone of her on the beach with the sun setting behind her. She was wearing a bikini.

"Very nice," John said. Of course, unknown to her, he was referring to her.

John began thinking more and more about Mexico and how much he liked it. He was already putting weight back on, and he just looked healthier. *Why not Mexico?* John was thinking.

"Well, I'm going to take a nap. I didn't sleep well leading up to this trip. I was scared and nervous," she said.

"Okay," John said. "Tonight, let's share a steak with *papas* and drink some beer, sound good?" John knew she liked beer because he had seen that she had bought a liter the night before, and hey, she was of German lineage.

"Sounds great," she said as she got up to retire for the afternoon. Her English was quite good for someone who had started learning it in high school.

That night, John and Katia had a great time together. They drank Barrallito Cervazas. She drank six herself, and John cooked the steak and potatoes. Then they smoked some marijuana. They had gotten the sequencing backward, but they were feeling no pain.

John showed Katia the book he had just written online on the publisher's website. John told her about the book and about his life of what the book was about.

She read a little bit from the book and asked John, "Where did you learn to write like that? It's so good."

"By reading," John replied.

"I want to stay in touch with you, so I'm going to ask you to be my friend on Facebook, okay?" she said, as she gazed into John's blue eyes through her blue eyes. She found John on Facebook and said, "Here you are. Nice fish you have there," referring to a picture taken when John had gone deep sea fishing with Darren off of Cape Cod so many years before.

"There, now just go to your e-mail and respond yes."

"I'll definitely do that we I get back online," John said, as he explained to her what had happened to his old laptop.

"Okay, well, you better," she said. "Your life sounds so interesting to me." Then she asked, "How old are you? Upper thirties, early forties?"

"No, older than that," John replied. "How old are you?" John asked, moving quickly to turn the tables.

"Twenty-one," she said.

Oh my god, John thought to himself. *What can I say, I've always had little boylike features with a man's body, it's always been that way. And I don't have a stitch of gray hair on my head, and my hair is totally bleached out blond from the sun, that's what this must be about. I owe it to my parents. God rest my dad's soul, and I trust my mother is still alive and well at the nursing home back in King's Port. Damn, she'll be eighty-nine years old this December, and I haven't seen her in over six years, and I probably will never see her again.*

"Maybe you can come and visit in Puerto Vallarta," she said.

"I'd like that. I just might take you up on that."

She was buzzed and having a good time. Her loose blouse easily showed her milky white, firm breasts and her short, white shorts easily showed her crotch, etched in a vertical crease of sweetness. She had her legs spread open halfway like a boy as she laid back in her chair with her head turned toward John, smiling and gazing dreamily into John's eyes. Her wavy blonde hair nestled down around her breasts.

The next morning, John and Katia had breakfast together on the veranda. Her flight was at three o'clock, so she needed to leave at around one o'clock. After breakfast, she asked Olga for directions to the airport, which John knew from the main highway coming into town but not precisely from there, only the direction, which was southwest of them. Olga told her in Spanish, and she then told John that it wasn't far and that she was going to walk there. "Olga said that it's only about five blocks away," Katia told John. John said that he would walk her there, which he did.

They left on time and she was the guide, as John hadn't understood the directions. Her bag weighed about twenty-five pounds, and of course, John carried it with its strap around his shoulder. And it was hot, very hot. She didn't really know where she was going, but they got lucky after walking past the baseball stadium on the left and the park on the right. They turned right, or west, down an avenue that led to the airport, which reminded John of the airport back in his hometown of King's Port. It was small with, maybe, two carriers servicing out of it, but it was nice and clean and air-conditioned. They must have walked about a mile, and John was hot and sweating, but he didn't feel tired. She invigorated him. But those blocks were like as wide and far apart as the avenues in Manhattan.

She went through screening and checked her bag while John waited to say goodbye. It was time for her to go to the boarding area.

"I had a great time with you," she said. "You were the silver lining to an otherwise miserable trip."

"Thank you," John said. "I had a great time too."

"Please write," she said as she was about to turn to go.

"I will," John said. "*Yo gustar tu*" were John's last words to her as he kissed her and she turned and left.

John had some loose ends to tie up in Belize City, and he asked Olga and Miguel to take care of Molly for him while he was gone. She agreed, probably reluctantly. He only planned to be away from Friday to Sunday. Earlier in the week, John had asked Olga about living in Chetumal and the cost of apartments. He told her that if things didn't work out in Dangriga, he might want to come and live there if that was feasible, given immigration laws, affordability, and the like. She told him she was also a realtor, and she would show him some apartments before he left.

John's main objective in Belize City was to pick up a brand new laptop computer that his good friend Christopher had sent for him from Connecticut. John's old, pawnshop-bought laptop of five years prior was ruined by water on the floor in his shoebox from hell almost three months earlier. He also had made an initial written formal complaint against Nelly and Frank with the Belize Tourism Board the day before he had departed for Chetumal but wasn't able to meet with the woman in charge who was out of the office that day. He wanted to go to meet her in person. John had noticed that the term *board* didn't give the feel of authority like maybe, "Belize Tourism Authority" or the "Belize Tourism Agency of the Federal Government" might have. He would be right.

The day before John left for Belize City, Olga did, indeed, take John to meet with one of her partners in crime—a middle-aged lady named Lolita, a real estate agent who John would later give the moniker of "Loco Lolita" because she rarely, if ever, did anything right or on time, as evidence thereof would soon become apparent. They walked up to San Salvador and turned left and to the entry to the apartments in back of the businesses facing the avenue. They were just a stone's throw from the Super Aki. Loco Lolita said that she was just a few minutes away, but they waited and they waited, and finally, Olga called her on her cell phone as she was pulling up in a van. She got out of the van and told Olga that she would be right back; she had to go and get the key. *I wonder why she didn't do that before coming here?* John thought.

She came back with the key, and they walked back through the gate and up the stairs to the apartment. At the top of the stairs, there was a vacant apartment on the north, or avenue side, and then a catwalk over the patio on the first floor, with concrete pillars about four feet high on the left but with no railing, to the furnished apartment. It was bigger than he had expected and had beautiful green tile floors and five windows; one facing west to the Super Aki, double-windows facing south out of the kitchen toward Olga's Inn, and two facing to the north from both the kitchen and the bedroom. A sixth window in the bedroom faced the west, mostly into to the back wall of the adjacent business. No windows faced to the east likely due to the residence next door. They collectively provided plenty of light and decent views of the surroundings. The kitchen had a two-eye gas-burning stove and a refrigerator and a sink within the tile counter top adjacent to the stove. John liked it a lot as he thought a bit more about it, and especially the price, an unbelievable two-thousand pesos a month, what comes out to about $3.60 per day, but he was thinking at the time that it might be something he would be interested in down the road if things didn't work out in Dangriga. John had always assumed that Mexico wasn't an option because of the language barrier, but his two-week stay there had convinced him otherwise. But John knew deep inside that Dangriga was a fairytale but a myth.

It took John less than twenty-four hours to come to the conclusion that there was no future in Dangriga and that the old lady, Mirna, was fantasizing about the whole thing. She probably was dreaming of having one more notch etched in her saddle before checking out. John wanted to learn Spanish, and he had a true friend in Olga. Also, the cost of living was much less and Chetumal was a real city, with real stores and restaurants, even Italian, and with real people.

On Friday morning, July 1, John went to the ATM on the far west side of the Super Aki and withdrew five thousand pesos, or about three hundred dollars, for the first month's rent, the security deposit, and a contract fee and gave the money to Olga to secure the apartment. He was then off on his journey, and what would turn out to be his adventure, to Belize City for the last time.

A Desperate Escape from Belize— Revisited

It was now the middle of September and John was completely fed up with Nelly. He contacted his bank back in Washington, Georgia, via e-mail (he still had no cell phone) and asked them to e-mail to him a pro forma bank statement from the date of his incarceration to the date of his release from prison. They did so, and John had reason to be angrier. It wasn't just the five hundred dollars that she had alluded to, but there were additional charges that totaled to four hundred and thirty dollars. There was a two-hundred-dollar charge at one gas station alone. And even a thirty-dollar charge with a dating service (that's fifteen US dollars, what a bargain). John was livid for obvious reasons. She had not mentioned a word of any of this.

He wrote her a letter itemizing the charges along with the accompanying bank statement, demanding an acknowledgement, an apology, and payment or at least a plan to do so. John got none of the above. Her only comment, when John had so accommodatingly offered her some relief, or credit, for taking care of Molly (not really) and the trip out to the prison, some eighty kilometers round-trip, she said, "A round-trip taxi costs one hundred and twenty dollars, not sixty." *What a bitch*, John thought. *She's truly an evil and vile person with no respect for the difference between right and wrong, and she has no conscience.* The battle lines had been drawn; living there could and would never be the same.

John's fifty-ninth birthday came and went, yet again, without any fanfare. Only an e-mail from Elisa wishing him a happy birthday.

Not even one from her mother, Jean, who only told Elisa to tell her dad happy birthday when they had spoken on the phone earlier. *She didn't want her fingerprints on it,* John thought. She was above that now, above John. *"Who died and lifted you up to perfection?"* The way John saw it, they were still both alive, so they were dead even, one way or the other. Even Christopher and Philip failed to check in on the old man. Did Alan wish him well? Maybe, John couldn't remember. Alan wasn't big on ceremony, only the moment. And certainly not Abby. She had drawn her line in the sand many months before. There was only Molly, six stouts on ice in a Styrofoam cooler, and Fox News.

John really liked Bill O'Reilly—a master at opinionated news delivery with style (he had seen him once at one of the dining rooms during his days at the Harvard Club in midtown Manhattan), and Megyn Kelly, smart and hot, and Sean Hannity, a good ole Atlanta boy with a great sense of conservative values. Day in and day out, they filled those lonely hours with provocative thought and interesting news in an America that had clearly seen her better days, and now ever more faintly in the rear-view mirror.

The weekend of October 18 rolled around and all hell broke loose. It started raining on Saturday, and by Tuesday, they had endured eighteen inches of rain in what was loosely described in the news as the "worst flooding in recent memory." Hey, guys, you keep records down here? Like record rainfall and the like? It's a glass narrow tube about ye -wide in circumference; surely, you've heard about it. It's been around for hundreds of years, or you didn't get the memo from Queen Elizabeth? She knew about it from her great-grandfather. Apparently not. Just word of mouth would be Belize's history. It was a tropical depression of monumental proportions, and nobody had even bothered to tell John about it.

On the Sunday evening news, the anchor, a woman of Belizean heritage, said, "Prime Minister Dean Barrow issued a statement early this evening, saying that this had been the worst flooding in the central and northern parts of the country in recent memory and that more significant rainfall was to be expected."

Wow, John sarcastically thought to himself, *that statement is loaded with information*. There were no videos of the floods or a split screen with her talking on one and footage from around the country on the other. No, just her sitting at a table reading the news with no varying angles or zoom-ins and zoom-outs. None of that stuff.

Frank knocked on John's door at about eight, evening time, on Monday, when water had begun breaching the door. He told John he needed to move upstairs for the night in room four—his old room. John gathered Molly, his laptop, and toiletries and headed upstairs, not knowing the half of what was emerging. All he knew was that it had been raining cats and dogs for days then.

Early the next morning, before anyone had awakened, John went downstairs to heat his water in the microwave for his usual cup of coffee. The rain had mostly subsided by then, but what he saw downstairs was astonishing. The hallway was submerged in about three and a half feet of water with his room on the right. The other two rooms happened to be unoccupied. *I wonder why?* John thought. *Not.* He waded through the water. First, to the kitchen, where he found the refrigerator floating on its front side down, a total loss. He then waded to his room to find all his clothes floating lifelessly among the filth and grunge.

It took a day for the flood water to subside, and it was then that John told Frank that his clothes needed to be washed. Frank told John that there was a good laundry down the road toward the K-Park grocery, another world-class operation to be commonly found in Belize. "Fuck, Frank," John concluded.

Damn, this place and all the self-centered assholes in it, John thought. And it was really true. Nobody in Belize really cared about anything or anybody but themselves.

But at least I'm back in my room, John thought. But on Friday, Nelly came to his room, and unlike before, she never entered but stood at the door and said, "Frank wants you back in the room downstairs by four o'clock."

"Tell Frank to go fuck himself," John responded, to which Nelly turned and left without uttering a word. Shortly afterward, Frank came to John's room and told John that he had to move downstairs, to which John replied, "No, I'm not moving. Get the hell out of here."

"Then I'll have to call the police," Frank said as he turned to walk away. Nelly was standing there, and she said to John, "Don't let that happen, you should move."

John reluctantly agreed because he could see himself back in prison, given the corrupt police in Belize. As he was moving his things back downstairs, he passed Frank on the stairs and said, "You fucked up," to what Frank only looked at him in bewildered fear, saying nothing.

In November, John had to deal with a long overdue surgery for his inguinal hernia that had been festering for almost a year then. He had to have all the tests redone due to his prison diversion and was, alas, scheduled for surgery on Thanksgiving morning.

John arrived that morning before eight to stand in line for that day's surgical guests. A black male teen stood directly in front of John and had a growth on his right ear lobe, about the size of a golf ball but not perfectly rounded, and what John suspected was the subject of his morning's activities. It was indeed, as they later sat in the surgical waiting area to be called in, among four others. He must have had it from birth, John suspected. *Just how hard it must have been for this young man to live life with such a visible albatross?* John wondered. *Yeah, my life sucks, but look at what an embarrassing misery that monstrosity must be for him? I bet his head feels tilted to the right just due to the weight of that thing. Today would be a special day for that young man and that was a good thing.*

John's doctor was a nice man from Nicaragua, and John was one of the first of a busy schedule of surgeries to be called in. He put on his patient robe and sat on the stationary cart on wheels, waiting to be wheeled into the operating room.

The wait didn't take long, and John was soon on the operating table with instructions from the nurses to crouch forward with knees and arms in a ball for an epidural. John thought those were only for women, but he was a thankful recipient of one that day.

The surgery went well, and John was home recovering by the evening. He called the guesthouse to ask Nelly to come and get him in her car because the epidural hadn't fully worn off, and he had no other reason to stay in the post-op recovery room. Her daughter answered the phone and said that she wasn't there, so John was taken downstairs and out front in a wheelchair to get a taxi. When he arrived a few minutes later, there was Nelly and the rest of her motley and disgusting family milling around by the front office as they always did; day-in, day-out, rarely making eye contact or speaking with anyone outside of the family. They spoke among one another in that stupid Creole English, as though they thought they possessed something that "foreigners" didn't have, the ability to speak where the rest of the world can't understand them. *Brilliant*, John thought. This great country, creators of nothing but sugar, mahogany, rum, and beer and not much else. There wasn't even a railroad in Belize because, John reckoned, there was nothing to ship from the mountains in the west or the beaches and cays areas to the south or the sugarcane fields to the north.

It had been John's second surgery in a third-world Caribbean country in his last eight years. That seemed pretty remarkable to him.

John finished writing his first book shortly after the surgery and spent December trying to select a publisher. He submitted his transcript to four so-called "vanity press" publishers, as it was seemingly the case that one must go to one of them to have a chance to be published. All four accepted the transcript, and John ultimately chose one out of New York City.

A gentleman from San Antonio came at the first of December, who John had met there at the guesthouse in the early months of his first year there. His name was Eugene, and he was originally from Belize. He had many relatives there and apparently always came back for the winter months. He was in his early sixties and was about John's height with jet-black hair. He looked a lot like Elvis Presley, which is probably why he liked to sit out on the front balcony on the second story in the evening and play songs by Elvis over and over. He was clearly an Elvis wannabe. He became a true friend of John's, as they liked to go out together to the Spanish nightclubs, where John always got the girls and Eugene served as John's wingman and seemed content to do so. The girls were always from either Guatemala, El Salvador, or Honduras, and they were always very young and some very beautiful. They would rush to sit beside John at the bar in hopes that he would buy them a beer. The problem John had with them is that they couldn't speak a word of English and he couldn't Spanish. But then again, John loved it because he could say anything he wanted to them for his and Eugene's amusement. Eugene knew a bit of Spanish, so he was able to answer questions they had about his American friend named John.

"Hey, baby, want to put a double lip lock on my love muscle?" John would ask them while he pointed down toward his crotch. They would return an awkward smile. Or another good one, "Would you like to take me into the ladies' room and have a little fun?" and John would point to the hallway leading to the lady's room. They would glance over their shoulder at where he was pointing, and then turn back around, all the while smiling. "You're not having your period, are you?" "What color are your panties tonight? Are they wet yet?" "Me no speak English," they would always say. It was all in good fun.

These nightclubs and bars were concentrated in the northeast quadrant of the city between West Landiver and Button Wood Bay, just north of the hospital. This area was probably the cleanest and safest area of town, along with King's Park to the south on the water where John had now lived for about two years, save for the prison stint.

John told Eugene all about that and Nelly, Ray, and Frank and what shitheads they were. Eugene didn't like it there because he thought it was too expensive, so he, being a local, set out to find more suitable living quarters.

Around the first of December, George Cook also arrived from Wyoming and moved in next to John. He was very friendly and generous and he liked Molly, which none of the shitheads living there did. Only Carlos had pet Molly the entire two years he'd been there. Not even the personality-less son of Nelly and Ray, named Ryan, and their obese twenty-year-old daughter named Jessica, who had just had a baby in September with, of course, no father to be found.

In the meantime, Eugene had found a place at a guesthouse in town just off the north side of the river on Front Street just to the west of the swing bridge. Eugene, who had already gone there to look at the available rooms, of which there were two, told John about the place and took him there in early January to have a look.

The guesthouse faced the river across the street, and there were shops all around and a beautiful church just to the east toward the bridge. It was a three-story wooden building that had obviously, at one time, been a private residence. The rooms, of which there were about six, were small but clean there on the second level. The upstairs contained a large kitchen with stainless steel appliances and—*Thank God*, John thought—a refrigerator with an ice maker. The community baths were downstairs on the first floor. They were shown the place by a black mother-son duo named Linda and Richard, who lived upstairs on the third floor. They seemed nice enough, and a room was four hundred dollars per month as compared to the seven hundred and fifty dollars John was paying then. They both agreed with Linda and Richard that they would move in in two weeks, and Eugene had bought a minivan, so moving would be a piece of cake.

John spent Christmas Eve at the Hour Bar drinking with the owner, Kevin. Kevin was of dual citizenship of both Belize and the United States. He had gone to college in Connecticut and had lost his father in a plane crash, of which he was the pilot, carrying an American couple to Ambergris Cay. He left a boatload of assets to Kevin, including the largest beer company in Belize, Belikin, and the distributor rights for Coca-Cola. John had been told by some that Kevin was the richest man in Belize. Kevin was probably in his early forties, John thought, and had been divorced with a couple of children living in Miami. They shared a bottle of champagne, compliments of Kevin, and somehow, the events of 9-11 came up. John told Kevin of the lawsuit between the owner of the building, Larry Silverstein, and his Swiss reinsurance employer, who had provided the lead—and most in terms of dollars—coverage on the buildings and property. John told him of his role as chief financial officer of the holding company, parent of the property and casualty sister company to John's company, the life and health reinsurer.

Kevin said to John, "You know, I hear all these stories about what you've done in the past, big-time stuff, and I see you living over there at that guesthouse and I wonder, is all this really true?"

John would never return to the Hour Bar his last six months there, although, in retrospect, he couldn't really blame Kevin. After all, it was a strange and enigmatic life John was living.

Eugene was kind enough to invite John over to his brother's house for dinner on Christmas Day. His brother was educated at Tulane University in New Orleans and his wife was from Cuba. She cooked a fabulous dinner of turkey and ham and stuffing and mashed potatoes and salad, while Eugene, his brother, and John sat out on the balcony drinking beer. The meal was just like back home many, many years before.

Eugene's brother lived in West Landiver, and the house was in a nice neighborhood just northeast of the hospital, where John had spent so much time. The house had an apartment, which was a converted garage with a bath and stove, a few chairs, and a bed, and his brother offered that Eugene stay there for free until he returned to San Antonio in early February, to which Eugene agreed, so it would be only John making the fateful move in the middle of January. Eugene picked John and Molly up first thing on that morning, and they packed all his things in the minivan and left, and all the while, Nelly watching from the front office, not uttering a word. John was relieved to be out of the Bayview Guesthouse. And he was sure that Nelly was relieved also to see him go. That day, too, he would receive an e-mail from his son, Alan, which was to be the last one he would receive from him for quite some time.

The first week or so at the North Front Street Guesthouse went well. His room was smaller than at the Bayview Guesthouse, and he had no private bath, but he was gone from a terrible situation and was saving money in the process. There was a large screened-in back porch with a table with three chairs and two additional chairs in the right back corner where most of the guests would gather around dinnertime and usually stay there until bedtime. The first prime minister of the newly independent Belize of circa 1981 had lived in the house just across the back of the property. The backyard was nice also, with a walkway of gravel lined by bamboo to a gazebo in the center of the yard.

John and other guests would sit out there in the evening, just listening to music, drinking beer, and talking. Most of the guests were passing through and stayed there for only a day or two—usually European. Two young men from the Netherlands were there for a two-day stop on their way down through Guatemala and Honduras, through Nicaragua and then on to Costa Rica. The three of them sat at the three-chair table by the screen, drinking beer, listening to music, and talking about Europe and the United States and politics and the like. They were young and liberal and naïve but fun to talk to because they were very nice and intelligent. This was only about a month and a half after the Charlie Hebdo attack in Paris by those goddamn radical jihadists. John told them that their people would learn that the world and the people in it weren't living in a utopia that they had imagined, and that there were many people with bad intentions out there, especially those assholes. He told them that he thought Barrack Obama was perhaps the worst president in John's lifetime; well, there was Jimmy Carter, but they weren't around for that.

He, Barrack Obama, had the financial acumen of a lapdog. And a lapdog he was to his progressive left-wing liberals, who desperately wanted a country of apologies for its past and submission and surrender to its future of potential continued greatness and good for all. He said that Treyvon Martin could have been his son, but not one of the hundreds and hundreds of black teens who had been gunned down in the streets of his adopted hometown of Chicago over the past several years of his tenure. No, they didn't meet the requirements of the political calculus. They couldn't possibly have looked like him. To him, they were faceless. No, they were killed by their own, and he didn't want to go there. What political gain was there in discussing that? This had nothing to do with him being black and John being white; this had to do with a charade that was all too clear to John. Thomas Jefferson wasn't rolling over in his grave; he was throwing up in it.

He did more to run up the country's debt, weaken its military, damage her relations with many once close allies, and destroy thousands of businesses than any president in the country's history, bar none. And what did he accomplish? You tell me. The young naïve men from the Netherlands seemed surprised by this revelation. They got a kick out of this conservative cowboy from America.

John had blown out another pair of flip-flops that week. It was always the same thing that broke; the thingamajig that you place between your big toe and the one beside it (John didn't think that toe had any particular name, but John thought it could be called the second biggest toe, and he just hadn't picked up on that) eventually and, as in this case, would break away from the flop's base. He had to go and report to immigration that week, so he wore his dock siders with no socks and set out on that long and dreadful walk. Before he was halfway there, the heel of his left shoe was rubbing the back of his foot raw. The sting with each step was virtually unbearable, but he couldn't walk barefooted as it would burn the bottoms of his feet, but he didn't want to go back to prison, so he pressed on. By the time he had completed his round-trip journey, he had a real problem on his hands. The blister was huge and bleeding. He had to walk up the street just on the southwest side of the swing bridge and buy another pair of flip-flops. Those were all he ever wore, and he supposed his feet were no longer accustomed to wearing regular footwear.

The couple staying in the room next to John were always there. They, like John, were staying on a long-term basis. The girl, John supposed in her early forties, was Caucasian and from Australia via El Segundo (which means "the second" in Spanish. John always wondered, *The second what?*), where she had been married to an American. She was pretty enough but, although John liked slim girls, she was too skinny. Her apparent boyfriend was a nasty looking Rastafarian from Belize. They liked to drink and smoke pot, and

God only knows what else. She liked John; she even cooked his dinner one night because she said she was concerned he wasn't eating enough. Sometimes, when she got tipsy and they were talking, she would touch John on his shoulder or his knee. Her Rastafarian boyfriend just sat over in the back corner and stewed.

On one of these nights after John had gone to bed, he was awakened by a knock on his door. He opened his door, and there was the Rastafarian.

"Leave my woman alone," he said.

"I don't want your woman, get out of here," John replied.

If she had been a bit more enticing, John would have taken her from him just out of principle and for retribution.

The next day, in the late morning, there was another knock, knock, knock on John's door. He opened it, and there stood six—yes, six—police officers with holstered pistols. All six were black; five men and one woman.

"Yes, may I help you?" John asked.

"We're going to search your room," one of them said.

"For what, what are you looking for?"

They didn't answer, and two or three of them came into his room and began going through all his belongings. In John's toiletry kit, one of them found a marijuana cigarette, what had been given to John by one of the other guests.

After they finished their illegal search, one of them said, "You're coming with us to the station."

"For what?" John asked, to which there were no replies.

John was whisked away in one of the two police trucks that sat awaiting them outside in front of the guesthouse. They soon arrived at a police station, but John didn't think it was the same one he had spent the night in some six months prior.

John was escorted upstairs to the chief of police's office. He, of course, was a large black man. John was sure he was going back to prison because of the marijuana cigarette, which they had brought back to the station.

It was a brief meeting. He called the FBI and, after their short conversation, called one of the officers into the room and said, "Take him back to his room at the guesthouse."

They had no warrant when they searched his room, but in Belize, anything went, especially when it came to the police. Linda and Richard had to have been aware that this was happening or had happened. They said and did nothing. There was no recourse, no path to justice for a private citizen or tourist to take. *At least I'm not going back to prison*, John thought as they drove him back to the guesthouse.

When John returned, he walked out into the back porch, where, of course, the Australian woman and the Rastafarian were sitting. John looked at the Rastafarian black man and said, "It didn't work, did it?" and continued walking to the back stairs and down into the yard where Molly had been kept in his absence. She was always happy to see her daddy. The Rastafarian man had no answer.

It was a beautiful night back in Chetumal, and John and Carla were listening to music at the front of her Estetica Carla salon. They listened to Loggins and Messina's *"Lately My Love"* and *"You Better Move On."* Then John played Sara McGlachlan's *"Building a Mystery"* and *"Sweet Surrender."* She said, *"Me gusta, mucho!"*

John had brought his notebook along with his laptop, where he had written down about thirty or forty songs that he wanted Carla to hear. On the first page of the notebook were a couple of paragraphs jotted down for his new book and a compilation of all the expenses for his trip he had taken back to Belize City for his final visit there. But mainly on the first page of the notebook were the Spanish equivalents for basic, everyday words in English, but she focused in on the compilation.

"You spent one thousand three hundred and fifty pesos at a bar? For yourself?" she seemingly demanded to know from John. She had told John that she didn't drink, so this wasn't a subject John wanted to dwell on.

"Well, most of it was on a woman," John replied.

"A woman? I can't believe it," Carla said. Then she thought about for a second and said, "Yes, I can."

"Tell me about your boyfriend back in Orange Walk," John said, quickly turning the tables back on her on a speculative hunch.

"What? Boyfriend in Orange Walk? Who told you I had a boyfriend in Orange Walk?" Carla asked.

"Nobody," John said.

"What do you know, and who have you been talking to?"

"Nobody," John replied.

"Tell me," she pleaded.

"I talk to no one."

"Then what, do you have telepathic powers?"

"No, I just know what I feel inside sometimes, it's nothing special. Call it a man's intuition, if such a thing exists. Why would you forget to do the one favor asked of you, and that was put one hundred pesos on my Belizean cell phone, and you forgot? One doesn't go to see only their aunt and uncle and forget such a simple thing."

They held hands and gazed into each other's eyes, both amazed and intrigued by what they saw and didn't fully understand.

"You're very, very smart," she said.

"No, not really, just perceptive, I think."

Then John played a song by who he considered to be the greatest guitarist of his time and possibly all time.

"This is Mark Knopfler, of Dire Straits fame, you know," he said and John sang, "*Get your money for nothing, and your chicks for free. I want my, I want my, I want my MTV.*"

He played "Telegraph Road" from the band's early days. She liked it very much, and it was putting her to sleep. She being a woman and all, as it was getting quite late.

"This is perfect for listening to during and after making love, it's a long song," John said. "It's an anthem of poetic beauty, of the soul and the human spirit, and the struggles in life we all face."

She rolled her eyes as if to say, "You're a bad, bad boy," and then looked back into his eyes and saw something she liked very much but had never come across before. She couldn't believe how this man had come into her life and seduced her so.

John couldn't count how many times a woman had called him a bad boy. *I wonder why? I'm generally a good boy*, John pondered the question and the answer dawned on him. Women like to be dominated by a man, at his mercy, preferably daily, to fully feel and appreciate their orgasms. What they're really saying is, "You're a bad (good, really), bad (really, really good) boy when you do that to me." Then it's back to business as usual.

John had been living in Chetumal for only a week and a half; well, three and a half, counting his stay at the Posada Inn, and he sensed he was already gaining a reputation. Many of the employees at the Super Aki smiled at John and always said *hola* and *buenos dias* or *hasta luego*, as he would be leaving—the women, that is. Passersby on the avenue gave a second look, especially the little ones. Other than at the Posada Inn, John hadn't seen a white person in Chetumal, although he knew that there were some there.

John told Olga the next day about Carla and Margareth—well, a little, anyway—and she said, "Watch out, you have sex with them and, to them, that is a commitment and they'll want a ring."

"No rings from this hombre," John said. "The train has already left the station on your other point, though."

Olga cracked up on that with her great laugh, which always made John laugh as well.

"You're going to break some hearts," Olga said. "Take your time, trust me."

John usually sat out on his patio or veranda overlooking San Salvador Avenue and Estetica Carla in the evenings. He watched her as she performed her work with great care and detail, and she had what looked to be a loyal customer base, albeit small, and business was slow in her salon as it was in most businesses, unlike back in the States. It appeared to John that her principal service was pedicures for women, and even some men, what John thought to be odd, as he watched her give them time and again there in the front and right-hand side of the store. She moved gracefully about the store in her shorts and blouse and tennis shoes with little white socks. Her body was so fine. And she was so ladylike yet so down to earth. Could it be happening? It wasn't her raw beauty that so intrigued John that she did not possess. But it was the way in which she was a woman, so different and unassuming and confident and happy in her own skin. And then there was the language thing, where they talked to each other in a mix of English and Spanish. It was very provocative and intriguing.

That very afternoon, when she had come over to see John, she was wearing a beautiful blouse cut at the armpits like a tank top, a gift from one of her cousins who lived in Toronto. It was gold and brown with hints of blue and was loose but scant, and John liked it very much. She didn't need to wear a bra; her breasts were somewhat petite but firm and fresh and as inviting—no, more inviting—as the sky above that beautiful evening. She then changed back into something like a tennis or golf shirt when she went back to work, which on that day happened to be red.

At seven o'clock, church bells chimed from the steeple to the north about a thousand meters—John could see the steeple from there—which probably stood about ten or fifteen meters tall, followed by the same to the south of Venustiano Caranza Street and the Posada Inn, where John used to hear those bells chime from the church to the south when he stayed there.

As evening was falling, the hues of colors of the sky, the clouds, the clothing people wore on the street, and the shop signs all became more and more vivid, as the brightness of the sun no longer contained all their true color and beauty. The trees lining the median of the avenue were palm, and there was another kind of tree, and they were fuller trees that looked as though the leaves were ferns one might find on the banks of the creeks and streams of the Smokey Mountains. On the opposite corner from John's veranda, and just to the east of Estetica Carla, was a tree with light, grayish bark that branched out into many branches jettisoning upward, holding what appeared to be a neatly manicured bush like that that you might find at the Biltmore Estates in Asheville. It looked like the fingers of that character in *ET* (what was his name, I forgot?), holding some sort of green sponge cake on a platter, only with more than five fingers.

Many kilometers to the north, high in the sky, were two massive cumulous clouds, one about four kilometers and the other about eight kilometers away, and whose collective apexes were probably around three thousand meters high. John was amazed at how they stood still for the better part of ten minutes and then quickly dissipated somewhat and lost their form as they moved to the north, inevitably succumbing in their attempt to soar ever higher. He had never seen such a thing, but then he had rarely sat fixated on clouds for ten minutes at a time. He had too much time on his hands clearly, but he was enjoying himself immensely.

When John was going back inside to get a beer, he saw the three-quarter moon at about ten o'clock in the sky as he faced south and as dusk had emerged, and he said to Molly, "Look at the beautiful moon tonight, Molly!" Of course, she didn't look up, and John realized that she probably had never seen the moon, at least not knowingly. *What a shame*, he thought. *It's a beautiful thing, and I couldn't imagine life without the moon.*

Speaking of the moon, John wondered if anybody had ever noticed that its sense of promptness was a bit lacking as displayed by its tardiness, as it continually showed itself in the sky later and later each night or day, by about thirty minutes or maybe an hour by John's estimation, until it started the process all over again. "*I don't*

know, it might be a little more time that it's tardy, or a little less, but it's nonetheless discernable. There's more thought and research on that needed. And I also wonder if the moon rotates like the earth does, or does it just sit like a motionless rock in space, only circling its master in a lemming-like, hypnotic state, oblivious to its inferiority. There's more research needed on that too, a lot more thinking to be done." John continued with his revelation, "*Yet it was a continuous circle, so I guess the process never starts over or ends, it just keeps on going.*" John concluded. "*It must be a continuous circle, just as life itself.*"

"*So let's think about this for a minute, or several. I have plenty of time. Given the earth is about thirteen times larger than the moon, the moon has no choice but to tag along and be subservient to its master. Well, anyway, the moon moves about the earth as both are locked in on their lateral motion. I believe it takes the moon about thirty days to complete its rotation around the earth, and there are about twenty-four hours in a day. So given a fixed position on the earth as yours and mine, the moon will appear, when it does appear, about forty-eight minutes later, each night and day, at roughly the same position it was the day or night before. Now I don't know if this is because the earth is moving eastbound at a faster rate of speed than the moon or what. I don't even know what direction the moon is going.*"

"*Who else had the ability and free time to sit around at night and think of such things?*" John pondered the question and concluded no one, except for mimes and the mentally impaired, and nobody really paid any attention to them anyway. John was sure that scientists and astronomers the world around would take note of his most recent and remarkable discovery. He also suspected that this phenomenon was caused by the fact—or theory, the physicists and astronomers would say—that they, they being both the earth and the moon, were indeed both moving at the same time and at different forward lateral and rotational speeds. But more research and reflection on his part was needed, especially on the forward and lateral stuff. It was a bit confusing. *I know there will be the skeptics, the pundits, and the naysayers, but I'll just have to prove them wrong by thinking about it some more*, John thought to himself. John was confident that something would come to mind. He was all but certain, and all but, were the operative words that he would be rich and famous for this revelation and someone needed to pinch him as he was sure he had died and gone to heaven.

"*And while we're talking about the earth, astrophysics, and stuff, here are a few things I know and a few that I don't, those of which will become obvious. The earth's rotational speed is about a thousand miles per hour. I know because I can feel the G-forces from time to time. And how fast is its forward lateral movement, you might ask? Or then again, you might not, but I'll answer the question anyway. Stay with me on this one, it's some serious, complicated stuff. Within the answers to these questions lie the secrets of life, and these questions and their elusive answers impact each and every one of our lives daily, I guess. And armed with the knowledge of the velocity of said earth, one can then simply take the derivative of said velocity, and therein lies the key to its origin, as in the earth's acceleration, but I think there might be some other variables in there that require further thought. Anyway, let's see, the median radius of the earth's rotational path around the sun is approximately ninety-three million miles, and it takes a year to complete the annual journey. Redundant, I know, but I don't really care because, you see, I work for the new federal agency, the Department of Redundancy Department. Well, actually, I'm on the payroll, but I don't show up for work, and I don't do anything except just duplicitous stuff, and I can never be fired. So by my calculations, that's pi-squared times a gazillion, then divided by, of course, the ninety-three million. You do the math. I just teed it up for you.*

"*What's that, you say? That's really fast? No shit, Sherlock. I could have told you that before I gave you the secret sauce. You're just wasting my time. Well, not really, I've got tons of that.*"

"*So much more to learn, yet so precious little time,*" John concluded, upon further reflection.

"*I got too much time on my hands.*"

John also found the city of Chetumal to be remarkably peaceful and orderly. There were no gangs on the streets or the homeless panhandling for their next drink; no groups of rowdy teens milling about. He felt like he lived in a small but elegant penthouse in Soho near the superb restaurant, One If By Land, Two If By Sea. John wondered if it was still there after all these years when he had dinner there with Jean and Samuel when they had taken Brandon to Mt. Sinai Hospital on the southern outskirts of Harlem on the Upper East Side of Manhattan twenty-seven years before.

He had only heard a couple of sirens the entire almost one month he had been there. The city reminded him of Alpharetta in its peaceful tranquility, only bigger in scale in terms of its being a city with a larger population. Alpharetta was spread out on a much larger scale but with less of a population, due to all its many golf courses and horse farms and office parks. Two different worlds, and each charming in their own way. Chetumal's population was that of about one hundred and eighty thousand people.

John and Carla listened to music in the front of the salon on Friday. One of the songs John played was "Angie" by the Rolling Stones. Carla said, "The Rolling Stones? Again?"

"What, you don't like them?" John asked.

"No, not really," Carla said.

"They're only the most popular band in the history of mankind," John said. "And they have written some of the best love songs ever. Yeah, the Rolling Stones have, who would have thought."

She then called John "Booboo," apparently because he had been misguided in his lofty assessment of the boys or, well, old men.

Just before darkness had fallen that night, a caravan of about eight to ten police and military vehicles, with their lights flashing, drove by heading east toward downtown. "What's that all about?" John asked Carla.

"It's Friday night. They go into town for the drugs, you know, cocaine."

One of the vehicles was a truck with an open bed in the back carrying a dozen or so soldiers dressed in camouflage green fatigues carrying military-style weaponry. *Pretty serious business*, John thought to himself.

On Saturday morning, John got up at six and did his usual routine. He opened the front door to another beautiful day in paradise.

He lit the stove for his first cup of coffee with milk and sugar, and then he brushed his teeth. He then did his usual rounds of push-ups, sit-ups, and arm curls. He used a cinder block for the arm curls. The bathroom was at about two o'clock relative to his front door and had about a six-inch elevation from the rest of the apartment. He would use that for his push-ups with his legs jettisoning out the front door. He laid a towel on the tile kitchen floor in front of the refrigerator and stuck his feet under it to do his sit-ups. He would then enjoy a second cup of coffee while daylight emerged from its slumber. He always left his front door open for the circulation of air it provided. He would then shower with the door open. It was as private as his beautiful house in Alpharetta once was to him. There was never a soul in sight to be found, no windows from other homes to be peered at through.

After his workout, John walked out onto his patio or veranda, and the sun was breaching the horizon about twenty degrees to the north of due east. The clouds in the sky were as still and placid as an infant, fast and sound asleep. The high cirrus clouds looked as though they had been pasted on a canvass of deep blue, motionless, it seemed, in their tranquility.

And now every morning when Molly got up, which was usually a couple of hours after John had, he would greet her by saying, "*Hola*, Molly, *me amor. Buenos dias.*" She didn't understand a word of it.

Today marks my first month of living in Chetumal and away from the misery known to me as Belize City, John thought. "What a difference a few simple choices can make in one's life. Coming to Chetumal instead of Dangriga and deciding to secure the apartment before returning to Belize City that one last time. You only get so many footsteps in life and the paths on which you take them, so choose them wisely," John often told himself. This was the first time in a long while that John had, indeed, chosen his steps wisely and the path on which they were taken.

John walked past the Super Aki to the west and got some pesos from the ATM and bought for Carla five pink roses. The heat was already staggering on that bright, sunny Saturday morning. Although it got hotter in Atlanta, the sun was so much more powerful there on the peninsula. John handed the roses to her as she was sweeping the walkway in front of her salon. She said they were beautiful and then handed them back to John, somehow thinking that he had bought them for himself. He handed them back to her and said that they were for here and gave her a kiss. She was happy.

He only had two thousand, three hundred and fifty pesos, or about nine dollars a day, remaining for the rest of the month due to his final four-day return trip to Belize City and the security deposit and contract fee on his new apartment. That wouldn't be a problem. Olga was going to the free zone that day to buy John two cartons of cigarettes for eighty pesos, or about three and a half dollars. His representative from his publisher in New York City had sent him an e-mail on Friday stating that the printing and binding of the books were complete and his ten copies were being shipped to Elisa in Stuart. John went back to his apartment and sat at the kitchen table taking, in thought, an inventory of things in general. He thought about how different he and Carla were and the pasts they had experienced. She was a country girl who loved country music, Americano style, and she was a hardworking, proud business owner. John had lived a life that she would sooner or later know of, and God only knows what her reaction to that past would be. He remembered how harshly she had reacted to his affair of many years before, and he liked that. If she only knew the rest, but that would not be a good thing.

"There's a fiction in the words between, just like telling stories. Sometimes a lie is the best thing."

She had morals, something that seemed rare to find in those days. John removed the cellophane and aluminum foil from his new pack of fifteen Delacados *cigaros* in 2.6 seconds, a new personal best. Life was good for the first time in many, many years.

That night, while they listened to music and watched the passersby, Carla told John that she would live with him if he would like, but she wanted him to stop smoking cigarettes and drinking beer. To that, John said no, that wasn't going to happen. She didn't put up a fight. She opened up so incredibly, it was amazing to watch her mouth and listen to her words, and the vulnerability that she must have felt at the time, the same feeling John had experienced so many times in the past with a woman, many different women. Her words flowed effortlessly and shamelessly like the water cascading over the cliffs of Niagara Falls. She was completely and innocently content in doing so; she had nothing to hide. She said that there were many women who would wish they were sitting next to him, if they had only seen and known him with such an opportunity as she had. She said to him that he was so handsome, and she couldn't believe he had been put into her life. She said she was so happy like never before, and it was all because of him. She said that she felt blessed and that it must be destiny, if it were to be so, she would be so lucky, and if not, John could break many hearts, and she was ready if one were to be hers.

John told her that he would see her the next night at his apartment on her day off and that she would wear a dress and put her hair down and wear earrings, something she didn't do while she was working. She said that she would, and that she would be there.

And there was Olga, who John was beginning to believe had been placed in his life by some god-like intervention. She had been the catalyst for all that now seemed at his fingertips. She was, indeed, a godsend.

Carla didn't show up that Sunday night, and John was shocked and upset about it. She had said just the night before that she wanted to live with him, although he didn't, or did he? "What is it with women?" John asked himself. "I think I know," he would conclude. "They are the ones that do or can carry a baby." But not John's. He had had a vasectomy over twelve years before, but of course, she didn't know that.

John left her a note the next morning while she wasn't in the salon on the table in front of the mirror. It read, "I try to love you, but you keep getting in the way. It's lonely without you, and it's lonely without me. I think I know why you didn't come last night. John."

Carla came to John's door the next day at noon and gave him some sort of sweet bun that she had bought from the grocery. John kissed her on the cheek and said, "I think I know why," and she nod-ded her head in agreement.

"What are we going to do about that?" John asked.

She said, "I'm sure we'll think of something. I've got to go. I have a customer. I'll see you tonight?"

"Yes," John said, and she glided down the stairs and went out the gate onto San Salvador Avenue.

"She's got a mind of her own, and she uses it well. Yes, she does, she's a one of kind. She's mighty fine."

Back at the North Front Street Guesthouse, John felt like he was in some sort of surreal horror movie, like *The Shining*,. At any time, one of those ghouls would jump out from a dark corner of the now haunted house and say, "Here's Johnny!" and then bellow out a deep and sinister laugh. John felt as though the Rastafarian man and Richard were surely out to get him. Richard didn't like Molly, or John, for that matter.

He dared not go out on the porch at night when the Australian girl and the Rastafarian man were out there. He was in another ter-rible situation in Belize City, where it seemed to be the norm rather than the exception. The Australian lass had taken John by the arm the following day to say that she was sorry when no one else was watching.

It rained that day with blustery winds that sent a chill to the spine, which was unusual for Belize, but it was the latter part of January, and even Belize could get chilly weather a time or two during January and February. That evening, Richard came and knocked on John's door.

"Your dog pissed on the floor up front by the door. We can't have that. Get a mop and go up there and clean it up," he said. "As a matter of fact, she can't stay inside anymore. She has to stay out back."

"Fuck you," John muttered under his breath as he began to gather Molly's water bowl and a towel to serve as a bed and blanket for her.

There were three other dogs living out in the backyard and under the house frame. One was that of the Rastafarian man and the other two were Richard's. They were all young and bigger than Molly, but luckily, they meant no harm to her. John took Molly out to the backyard at about ten o'clock where, luckily, the rain had stopped. But it was unusually cold. He hated this situation for Molly, and he hated the asshole, Richard, who had caused it. Shit happens, you know, and it wasn't even shit but piss. Big fucking deal.

John went to bed at about midnight but was quickly awakened by the distinct sound of Molly crying. His stomach felt butterflies and his mind felt anger as he got up and took a towel with him, where he found Molly at the bottom of the stairs, shivering and petrified. *Fuck this*, John thought to himself as he picked her up and carried her up the stairs and back inside to his room and into his bed. *She's far too old to endure this kind of nonsense*, John thought as Molly was soon warm and fast asleep.

At about midmorning the following day, someone came and knocked on John's door. He opened and there stood a policeman, black, of course, they all were. For that matter, the prime minister was black, the city councilmen were black, all the judges and police officers in Belize City were black, although statistics alleged that Belize City was about half black and half Hispanic, with a sprinkling of Taiwanese and Chinese. It made no sense.

"You're going to have to leave the guesthouse," was all he said. Then gesturing for John to follow him onto the back porch where Linda sat waiting by the table by the screen.

"You brought your dog in from the outside last night after you were told she couldn't stay inside."

"She was crying, it was cold," John said.

"Well, we're going to have to ask you to leave. Here's one hundred and fifty dollars that you paid for the remainder of the month," she said in a business-like fashion, a cold-hearted bitch of a woman. The policeman sat at the table with them in silence. Richard was nowhere to be seen.

"When you are packed and ready, we will have someone from off the street help you carry your things out to the front and for a taxi, I presume," she concluded.

"Okay, I don't want any trouble," John said as he got up from the table and headed back to his room to pack. Soon a young black man came to his room to help John with his things. John had his duffle bag packed, he thought, and then there was a cooler and his briefcase with his laptop, and of course, Molly and her traveling cage.

"What about this cooler?" the young black man asked. There were odds and ends in it like a coffee cup, a knife, and a plate. "You can keep it," John said as they headed out to the front with the rest of his things.

As they loaded his things into the trunk of the taxi, and Molly into the back seat, John was wondering where in the hell to go.

As they headed southeast toward the swing bridge, the taxi driver asked, "Where you headed?"

"The Bayview Guesthouse," John replied. He couldn't think of anywhere else to go. *What a nightmare*, John thought, as he was wondering if Frank would even let him and Molly stay there.

John and Molly got out of the cab and the driver helped with the luggage. Carlos was soon at the gate to greet John and asked him where he had been. John said, "I'll tell you all about in a bit. Is there my room for me and Molly?" Carlos said sure, and they were back in their room, a respite from a nightmare.

Carlos helped John carry his stuff to his room, and John said, "I need a beer. Here's ten dollars, go and get us four beers, can you do that?" to what Carlos was always up for. And then he told Carlos all about what had happened. Carlos was enraged. He said he was going to go and put a bullet in their heads. "Easy now, Carlos," John said. "You don't even own a gun." He was relieved to be back but realized in the back of his mind that he didn't want to be there either. He had nowhere else to go.

The next morning after showering, John went to his duffle bag for a change of clothes. He was shocked and dismayed to find that he had none. He had left all of his day-to-day clothes, which were the only ones in life he had, back at the North Street Guesthouse in a two-drawer chest. Also, his tennis shoes that Willie, Elisa's boyfriend, had given him before leaving Stuart. They were in the backyard drying out from all the mud and rain from the past couple of nights. Carlos was there and offered to ride on his bicycle to get his clothes. John was glad it wasn't him who was going but didn't have a good feeling about the foreseen outcome. Carlos came back in a half an hour and told John that Richard had told him that John had given all his shorts and t-shirts away. Asshole. What a liar. "Who in their right mind would give away their own shorts and t-shirts, one's everyday stuff?" John rhetorically asked Carlos, to which he had no answer. John had the one pair of shorts that he was wearing and a bathing suit and a few extra t-shirts, the ones that he least liked. Goddamn Belize City and all the wretched souls who lived within it.

George was a good friend and neighbor during those awful days. He bought for John antibacterial ointment for his badly blistered left heel, gauges and tape, Band-Aids, and even earplugs for those dreadful nights when the music from the BTL (Belize Telephone and Light) stage in the park or the bar on the corner behind the guesthouse, Thirsty's, was so loud and repetitious that it could drive one mad.

John spent much of February and March working with his publisher on editing his book. That was good fun for John, taking him back to his days in insurance and reinsurance and the myriads of different contracts and Securities and Exchange Commission filings that he had reviewed and constructed with his legal brethren. Abby and Elisa's birthdays were in February; Abby, her twelve years now complete, and Elisa, a milestone of thirty years. John didn't bother sending Abby a card, whose line in the sand had been drawn, and he would just have to wait for his ability and opportunity to make reparations with his sweet daughter Abby.

In early February, a young girl of about twenty years came and moved in, initially with Carlos and his girlfriend, Maria, and Maria's daughter, Fatima, who were both from Honduras. Carlos's girl, Maria, and him were a bit of a *Harold and Maude* type of relationship; you know, the movie. Carlos was about twenty-four years old and Maria's daughter, Fatima, was in high school there in Belize City and was about seventeen years old. Fatima was a very pretty girl, very petite and very feminine with an exceptional face and body to match. So do the math. John reckoned Maria was about forty years old, but her face looked older.

Then someone tapped John on his shoulder. It was his inner conscience. "Why does Carlos and Maria's relationship seem so strange to you? You've been doing the same thing for over twenty years now."

"I get it, you have a point," John said back to his inner conscience or, for the most part, his better half. These pesky little double standards, always getting in the way, John thought to himself.

Anyway, the young girl, whose name was Lisa, had come to stay along with her four- or five-year-old son with Carlos and Maria for a few months. Neither spoke a word of English, as Maria didn't either. Fatima, however, spoke it very well. Lisa was Maria's niece, and she was lean with a nice face and body with hair of a gold-like color. About a month later, she moved into the room next to Nelly, and soon after, another girl from Honduras moved in with her, but her son stayed in the room with Carlos and Maria.

Seems a bit of a strange and complicated situation, John thought, but both of the very attractive girls now lived in the room directly across from his in the old building. Turned out, they both had gotten jobs at the Latino bar that John and Eugene had visited a few times. So they would usually come home at about three in the morning, so John figured that her little son stayed with Maria and Carlos because of that.

Lisa liked John—he could tell by the way she looked at him, but they had no means of communicating. It was frustrating for John because she seemed nice and was a pretty young girl. But they talked with their eyes. Lisa might be sitting on the steps leading to the rooms on the second floor, and John would happen to walk by, and she would reach out and grab his hand and smile. Or John might tweak her on the cheek while she talked on the phone. One afternoon, John and George were in their hallway by the kitchen, and she came out of the shower of the older building across the way to go into her room, wrapped in only her bath towel. She stopped at her door and saw John and waved. George said, "Damn, son, what did you do to deserve that?"

"Nothing, absolutely nothing," John replied.

Every couple of months it seemed, John would get depressed about his lot in life and go out a buy a bottle of rum to ease the pain. It proved to do anything but. On this particular occasion, John was trying to get the plastic seal off the bottle with his right incisor, the coveted one that. as a young boy, he used to turn a McDonald's straw into a perfectly uniform slinky, and a piece of the plastic broke off between the coveted incisor and his right front tooth. John tried to remove the plastic with his scissors, brilliant as it were, and he popped the tooth out. His most cherished tooth was now gone, and he couldn't afford to pay for a bridge. Now John smiled with his lips sealed tight. But that was okay because he didn't smile that often those days.

In early March, Nelly came on one late Saturday morning with a new car, which was a smaller car, a Suzuki, of all things (John thought that they only made motorcycles).

John said to Nelly, "That's great! I see you finally sold your car."

"Well, I really just traded mine for this one."

"Well, that doesn't do me any good."

"I'll see what I can do," she said.

She came to John's room a short while later and gave him one hundred and fifty dollars. That would be all she would ever pay him back. Bitch.

In mid-April, John started communicating online with a lady who lived in a small village in the south of Spain near the entry point connecting the Atlantic Ocean and the Mediterranean Sea. They shared many photographs and sent e-mails daily; sometimes as many as twenty or so a day. Her name was Elena Vegas, and she had long golden hair and a nice, toned body. She was in her midforties and was divorced with two teenage sons. She seemed the perfect age for John and had children as he did and had been through two divorces as he had. She rented space in her house to foreigners visiting in Spain and also worked for an American couple as a tutor for the Spanish language and caretaker thereof as the parents were there abroad working. They became very interested in one another, and she asked John to come and visit her. She told John that she was in love with him and that she didn't want to lose him and that if he would please come, everything would be so good. *Really? What then?* John thought. John had heard this before. Women are so quick to say they love you, and then the next day, they won't give you the time of day. Why is it so about women?

She would wake up in the morning to John's final e-mail from the day before and tell John that "It was like opening Christmas presents every day." They told each other many things about their lives and became quite close, if that's possible with someone you've never actually seen or touched.

They talked about sex and what they would do to each other when they finally met. In the kitchen, in the bathroom, all over the place, in explicit detail. And then she would tell him that she had just masturbated twice while they were in between e-mails, thinking of him and looking at his picture, feeling his forceful penetration from behind. Then she would kneel between his legs, spreading them wide apart, whether in bed or in the kitchen or the bath, and bend her head down and slip it into her mouth, one hand firmly yet gently around its throat.

Their relationship, of what neither could see how it could move forward, lasted until about the first of June and ended abruptly, as all relationships with inanimate objects tend to do. One wonders how such relationships can get started. No, on second thought, one doesn't.

That was about the time that George found another stray feline, a Hispanic girl named Zulme. She was sweet, and George didn't deserve her because he kept bringing back to his room other stray felines, mostly blacks. The three of them liked to go to the pool around the corner at the Pickwick Club, which was directly across the street from the park on Princess Margaret Boulevard.

They would drink beer and jump in the pool every so often and enjoy the sun and clear blue skies. One particular Saturday, when the three of them were there, a Latino woman was sitting a couple of tables over with another black couple. She kept staring at John and smiling at him. George said, "Go on over there and introduce yourself to her, you dumb ass. It's obvious she wants you."

So John did, and after introducing themselves to one another, she asked John where he was staying. He told her, and she said she would like to come over that night. John said okay and that he was in room seven on the ground floor. But she never showed up, as so often is the case, but it's like in baseball; if you bat over .300, it's all good.

Oddly that following Tuesday morning, while John was having some coffee at about eight o'clock, Carlos came to his room and said to John, "There's a girl out front looking for you." John walked out of his room, and there she was, the girl from the pool, standing there with a backpack on. She was a nursing student in Belmopan and likely stopped by to see him before getting on the bus for school. John couldn't remember her name, which was all too common. *What a strange time to come to be with someone you don't even know*, thought John as he greeted her and asked her to come in. John didn't know if she had come to have sex or what, so he did the gentlemanly thing and told her he was getting ready to walk downtown with George, which was true, and that they should exchange e-mails so that they could get together, to which she obliged.

"Women do strange things, don't they George?" he said as they strolled, or at least John did, as George hobbled along past the Princess on their way into town.

"Don't ask me about women," George said. "Do you really think I know anything about women and what makes them tick? You're asking the wrong person. Trust me, I learned that many years ago."

Zulme and George had a falling out of some sort, and she stopped coming by. John didn't really press George on the matter because it was easy to see when he didn't really want to talk about something. He'd just say, "John, I told her that she's too young for me, and that she's got her whole life ahead of her. Go find a young man who can treat you right." That was only part of the truth, John was sure, but it didn't really matter.

That's when Mae started showing up more and more. She was a very nice lady but apparently not very smart. She had had ten children with no man to claim them.

One morning in early June, John walked downtown to meet her at her house so that she could go with him to help buy a phone and get phone service. They did so, and for the first time in over two years, John had a cell phone.

Later that afternoon after John had returned to the Bayview Guesthouse, Mae showed up at his room with her second youngest daughter, Anisha, and another young girl who was somehow related to the two, but John wasn't sure how. Anisha was very attractive physically. She was built like a gazelle. At about five feet and seven inches, she was long and lean and only seventeen. As John recalled, the older girl had told him that she was twenty-one. They all piled into John's tiny room; Anisha and the other girl on the bed with John, while Mae sat on the foot-high step to the bath. Mae asked John if he would buy them lunch from the park, to which John obliged. Mae had been most helpful earlier that morning, so John had no problem feeding them.

After they ate, they just talked, and Mae was kind of waiting for George to come back from wherever he was. They younger ones started asking John questions as they were all three squeezed onto the bed. The older of the two asked, "Where's your woman? Don't you have a woman?"

"No," John said. "It's just me and Molly."

"Don't you want somebody to cook for you and rub your back and make love to you?" the twenty-one-year-old asked.

"Well, yeah, I guess that'd be nice, but it just hasn't happened," John said. *I wonder if she's applying for the job?* John thought to himself.

Anisha said, "Take your shirt off, and I'll give you a back massage."

John took his shirt off, and she gave him a wonderful back massage, one of which he hadn't experienced in years. But it was a bit awkward that this seventeen-year-old bombshell was giving it to him with her mother watching, not to mention the other one.

About that time, George wandered in from one of his many and frequent runs through the jungle, that being the streets of Belize City. Mae asked George if he would come back with them to her house, to which he agreed. They decided to go down to the Chinese market by the basketball courts and get a beer while they waited for a taxi. John went along but didn't intend to go with them back to Mae's house. As they were walking out, Anisha said to John, "I'm going to come over tomorrow afternoon to see you, okay?"

An Enigma

The Day John's Shorts Caught on Fire

They—John, George, and Mae—drank their beer, and the cab soon after arrived. It was scorching hot at about one-thirty in the afternoon, as John said so long and headed back to his room. About halfway back, John felt a stinging sensation on his right hip, right around the pocket of his shorts, and smelled something burning. He pulled his shirt up, and lo and behold, his shorts were on fire. He quickly patted it out with his hand and shirt and wondered, *Holy shit! What just happened?*

John had nothing that day in his shorts' right pocket. No money, no lighter, no matches—absolutely nothing. He had burn marks just to the left of his right hip to provide the evidence, but no one really cared. To which George said, "Really?" Clearly, George had to be thinking to himself, "Yeah, right." To this day, John considers it to be the eighth wonder of the world. Step aside Astrodome. *Could it have been a stand-down order from above regarding Anisha?* John wondered. She was actually only sixteen, soon to be seventeen in late July.

Speaking of stand-down orders, John couldn't help but think of the nonsense going on back in the States with Hillary Clinton. Would James Comey, the director of the FBI, conclude that there was not enough evidence to indict Hillary Clinton for numerous felonious violations regarding the improper handling, dissemination, and storing of state department classified information? Right in the middle of a presidential election, you ask? He sure would. Courtesy of a direct dictum from the president. What a joke. A sad state of affairs, to be sure.

It was almost the middle of June, and John saw no future at all in Belize City. He needed to get the immigration albatross off his neck, so he decided it was time to leave for Mexico, not realizing at the time that it might be for good.

"So that's an awful story," Olga said to John. "I can't believe you stayed there so long and around the most terrible of people. But now you're here in Mexico, and you're going to have your own apartment right around the corner from me and none of those evil people to worry about."

"Yeah," John said, "I just have to make this one last trip there and then it's all over. The final chapter will have been written."

Belize City

The Final Chapter

It was Friday, July 1, and John was up bright and early as usual and ready to embark on his journey to Belize City, now knowing that it would probably be his last. He went to the ATM and got five thousand pesos to give to Olga for securing the apartment. When he got back to the Posada Inn, Olga was up, for a change, and sitting at her computer.

"Are you all set to go?" Olga asked.

"Yes, here's the five thousand pesos," John replied as he gave her the money.

Olga counted the pesos in bills, and it only came to four thousand five hundred. *Damn, that's strange*, John said. *I distinctly remember asking the damn machine for five thousand. I guess I'll have to go back.*

Time was running short as John needed to get to Belize City by two-thirty to three o'clock at the latest if he was going to be able to retrieve his new laptop and walk across town to the computer store on Baymen Avenue. They would then have to transfer all his files from his deceased computer to his new one. Luckily, the files were recoverable and contained the only photographs he had left in this world. John went back to the ATM and withdrew three thousand more pesos. He didn't know why he had gotten so much since he would be in Belize shortly and would need Belizean dollars. It would turn out to be very fortuitous that he got so much. Call it a man's intuition—not. Just luck, he would later guess.

When John returned, Olga said, "You didn't give me instructions on Molly."

"I told Miguel. She needs to go out about four or five times a day, and usually she'll let you know when she needs to go by walking to the door. Otherwise, she eats two or three times a day with a little something extra poured over the dog food, like tuna or frijoles," John said. "She'll sleep by the door of your bedroom, as we discussed, in my duffle bag with my clothes in it so that she has the comfort of my scent. That's about all there is to it. Bye, Molly, Daddy will be back."

Miguel was Olga's housekeeper and general handyman. He was a very nice man of twenty-nine years and had come from Mexico City only weeks prior to John's arrival. He was a bit shorter than John and on the thin side and balding on the top and was a soft-spoken gentleman who knew English well, like Olga. He lived in a room on the third floor, where John had not been before. Every morning that John stayed there, Miguel cooked either pancakes or scrambled eggs and bacon, with potatoes or grilled vegetables or both, and grilled bread for the two of them, while Olga was almost always still in bed. She was a night owl if there'd ever been one. John was quickly gaining back desperately needed weight lost from his hell in Belize.

After John had given Olga the money for the apartment, he walked up to the front of the Super Aki and waved a taxi over to the side. They headed west past the airport and were there at the border in a short fifteen minutes. They pulled up to the border crossing agents' checkpoint, and the taxi driver got out of his car and accompanied John. There was another Mexican there who knew English and was assisting people like John.

"Your passport, please," the agent in the little checkpoint office said.

John gave the man his passport, and then the man assisting asked, "Where's your data card you filled out when you entered the country?" the man asked John.

"I don't know, I don't recall getting one," John said.

"Yes, you filled a duplicate copy out on a perforated form, and they gave it back to you for when you were leaving the country."

"Let me check my folders in the taxi, but I don't recall that," John said.

John went back to the taxi and looked to no avail.

"I don't have such a thing, *no pongame*," John said.

"You're trying to leave the country illegally, you could get a summons to court," he said.

Oh swell, now I'll get locked up in Mexico, John was thinking to himself.

The man assisting John, the taxi driver and the border agent, huddled, and the English-speaking man made a brief phone call, from which he returned to John and said, "Can you pay the exit fee of three hundred and thirty pesos?"

"Sure, yes," John replied.

"Okay, you're good to go," he said. "Just pay at the window, and he'll take you to the Belizean customs area." By he, he meant the taxi driver.

John paid the exit fee and was cleared from Mexico, and on to the Belize customs and immigration side. That's when he met the bus driver who told him about the gentlemen's club in Chetumal. It was called Aracifus, which means "the reef." As they headed down the narrow two-lane highway to Corozal, John told the driver that he needed to go to an ATM because he had no Belizean dollars. The driver said, "Okay, there's a bank two blocks down in the center of town, but hurry if you want to catch the eleven-thirty bus to Belize City. John walked and trotted and got there very quickly. He put his card in the machine and asked for four hundred dollars, which is what he thought he would need to pay the damn Belizean government two hundred and ninety dollars, an import tax if you will, and the rest of his anticipated expenses for the two-day trip. The machine didn't give him a dime—why, he wasn't sure, but then he started thinking about his maximum allotted daily withdrawal amount that had caused him problems the day he went to court that one long year before.

Damn, I think that's the problem, John thought as he hurried back to the bus driver, who was waiting at the bus terminal. "*Let's see, if the limit is still five hundred dollars, Belize, per day, how much does the eight thousand pesos I just withdrew in Chetumal come to?"*

John asked the bus driver if he would take pesos because the machine didn't work for some reason, and luckily, and probably without an alternative, he said okay. He gave him one hundred and twenty pesos, which was about twelve dollars, and covered the ten-dollar ride. It was ten dollars from the border to Corozal and another ten dollars the near one hundred miles to Belize City.

As the eleven-thirty bus left the station, John was relieved that he had made it. He then started converting pesos to Belizean dollars in his mind as the bus rolled south through town with the beautiful Corozal Bay off to the left. *"Let's see here, I got three thousand pesos out of the ATM, and I gave Olga an additional five hundred, and I paid the Mexican exit fee of three hundred and twenty, and I gave the bus driver another one hundred and twenty. Oh yeah, and I also paid the cab driver one hundred and twenty. That should leave me with two thousand four hundred and forty pesos. Let me check. Yes, exactly. Good, now how many Belizean dollars, or US dollars, for that matter, did I take out?"* John calculated that he had withdrawn about four hundred and eighty US dollars, which was nine hundred and sixty Belizean dollars, which was well over his limit of five hundred Belizean dollars. In fact, he was surprised that he was able to exceed his limit, but now knew full well that that is what had happened. *Maybe their software couldn't calculate any faster than me. We'll see,* John thought. *I'll go to the bank in Belize City and convert these pesos to dollars, shouldn't be a problem.* He happened to have fourteen Belizean dollars leftover from when he had come up to Chetumal, which covered the bus fare of ten dollars.

The bus pulled into the station in downtown Belize City at three o'clock sharp. John hurried onto the street carrying only the backpack that Olga had lent him. He turned right onto Orange Street exactly how he had done two and a half years before, heading to the Caribbean Palms Hotel, which was on Legion Street just south of the courthouse he had the pleasure of appearing at one year before. He thought he would check in using his bank card and then head farther south three or four blocks to the Belize Tourism Board to meet, hopefully, with its head lady. He thought the hotel was forty-three Belizean dollars, but the clerk told him that it was forty-three US dollars and that they didn't take credit cards. So, never surprised by disappointment in Belize, John left and headed to the tourism board's office. He was lucky and the head lady was there and available, and they met in a couple of chairs in the lobby, as all the offices were being used. John told the head lady—her name was Vanessa (black, of course)—the sequence of events that last summer with Nelly and Frank. He gave her a copy of the letter that he had written to Nelly in December, and he gave her a copy of the pro forma bank statement with all the charges she had made during his visit to the prison. Vanessa told John that they would address the issues with Nelly and Frank, but first, her internal legal counsel needed to review the matter. John also told her of how Frank had had all his things removed from his room in June while the room had been paid for and what resulted in the thievery perpetrated by Carlos.

Satisfied at the moment with their meeting, John left their office and walked quickly back into the heart of downtown and then across the swing bridge toward the post office across from the water taxi on Queen Street. He walked up to the door of the post office, and there he saw their hours posted on the door. It read, "Monday to Thursday—8:30 to 4:30. Friday—8:30 to 3:30." They were closed, but the door was open and several clerks were still there.

"I've come to pick up a package, a laptop computer," John said.

"We're closed already, but packages are kept around the corner. Just go there and ask the supervisor, he'll probably let you pick it up," the black male clerk said.

John went out and around to the separate building and went inside, where—yes, you guessed—the black male supervisor was standing behind the glass-protected counter. "I'm here to pick up a package from Connecticut. It's a laptop computer," John said.

"Yeah, we've got it. It's yours for two hundred and ninety dollars," the supervisor said.

"How about a credit card?" John asked. He knew he had exceeded his limit for the day, but that was just for ATM withdrawals, not vendor purchases.

"Nope, only cash," he replied.

"You've got to be kidding me?" John said, not asked, as that, too, was a rhetorical question. "Nobody in this country takes credit cards, not even the goddamn government," John said, as he was clearly frustrated.

"You can run over there to the bank and get the money, I'll wait," the supervisor said. John knew that wouldn't work, but he had remembered the day he went to prison that in order to get the second five hundred dollars, he went to Scotia Bank and they did a cash advance for an extra twenty dollars. He guessed his bank treated that as a vendor purchase.

I'll do that, John thought to himself as he bolted out the door. *But I'd better hurry. It's already four thirty-five."*

John went to the foreign exchange counter at the Bank of Belize, and the woman behind the counter told him that he had just made it in time and that she would be happy to do that for him.

Thank God, John thought to himself as he handed her his card, and she walked away to process the transaction. She soon came back and handed John his card and said, "It didn't go through. You might want to try another bank."

Now panicked, John went to two other banks, one across the street and another a couple of blocks south of Brodie's. They were both closed.

John went back to the postal package office and asked the supervisor if they would be there the next day, which was Saturday. He said yes, that somebody would be there at nine to give him his laptop. John thought, or was really hoping subliminally against hope, that his card would work the following morning.

John walked out onto Queen Street and didn't even have a room for the night. He had no Belizean money either. He headed east to the intersection of Barrack Street and Queen and went into the corner grocery, which was owned and operated by an Indian from the east. He went inside and asked the gentleman where there might be a room for the night.

"There's the Sea Breeze Guesthouse a few blocks over toward the sea, or just right there, above the electronics store, is the Three Sisters' Guesthouse. Just walk over there and ring the buzzer."

"Okay, thanks," John said as he thought he'd try the Three Sisters place as it was right there and just around the corner from the internet café that he had been using so frequently since his computer died. He rang the bell, but no one came. He rang it several more times until he gave up. Businesses in Belize City opened and closed as their owners saw fit, and on that day, the three sisters apparently had better things to do.

John walked down Queen Street farther to the east and zigzagged his way down two streets and passed Mae's house (George's most recent stray feline) and, there on the left a couple of doors down was the Sea Breeze Guesthouse. The front gates were locked, but a man came out from the garage area underneath the guesthouse and said to John, "We're closed."

Unbelievable, John thought, as was a beautiful Friday evening and these two had better things to do. He decided to go to the internet café and ask the man who owned the internet café if he knew of anyplace that had a room for the night.

"Try across the street and up a few doors, there's a hotel there."

"Thanks," John said as he headed out the door and across Queen Street to the alleyway that led to the Tourist Village. The gates were locked as he asked a man next door about the hotel.

"It's been closed for a while," the black man said.

John went back into the corner grocery and was stunned by what he saw. He saw, standing in the aisle directing in front of the counter, quite possibly the most beautiful girl he had ever seen. She was probably in her midtwenties and had long black hair and an immaculate body, shaped to perfection—every curve and subtlety of her body was exquisite. Her breasts were firm and upright and the most perfect of sizes. She had dark brown eyes and the nose of Cleopatra. Her mouth was perfectly formed and so inviting. She wore a tightly fitted dress skirt that was grayish-blue, and her blouse was silky cream. One could only imagine how sweet and delicious her love nest was. She came to the counter to check her things, and John asked her, "Do you live around here?"

"Yes," she said.

"Do you know of any rooms for the night that are close by?"

"No, sorry, not really. I'm new here."

John wanted to ask her if he could sleep on her couch for twenty dollars, but then thought the better of it. He could envision a scene right out of the movie, *Dumb and Dumber*, where John says to her, "There's twenty dollars in it for you, and there's more where that comes from." She laughs and says, "Fat chance," to which John says, "So you're telling me there's a chance? Yes!" She left with her hand-ful of purchased items, and said, "Goodbye," as she headed down Barrack Street and went inside the internet café.

Damn, what a sight for sore eyes, John thought as he followed her to the internet café, not because he was stalking her but because he had a good reason to go back, and that was to ask the gentlemen inside if he knew of any other places to stay that night.

I wonder where she is from? John thought. She can't be Belizean but stranger things have happened. She looked to be European or maybe Italian or from Spain. She had the beauty and elegance of Angelina Jolie. *Where was she the whole fucking two and a half years I was here? Get over it*, John thought to himself. *You have to find a place to sleep tonight, and it won't be at her place, wherever that may be. I wish I knew, though.*

She went to one of the computers on the far wall as John came into the café and asked if he had any other places in mind.

"Yes," he said as he swiveled in his chair and pointed slightly down and across the street. "You see that beige building? The guy there has a couple of rooms upstairs."

"Thanks," John said as he walked out the door. He would prob-ably never see that most beautiful of creatures again.

He crossed the narrow street and the owner was in the entryway. "Do you have any rooms for the night?" John asked him.

"Damn, hell no, I just rented it, and I wish I could rent it to you instead of them." Then he glanced across the street and to a balcony behind a tall building on the opposite street side and shouted out, "Hey, Molly, do you have a room for the night?"

"Yes," she shouted back.

I'll be damned, John thought to himself. *There's the same Molly that I met about a month ago when Mae took George and me to see her place and see if there were any rooms available.* John really liked the place, although he hadn't actually been inside any of the rooms, as they were all taken at the time. He called Molly and texted her several times before leaving for Chetumal, but she never really responded, just a text he received back initially with the following content: "???"

Molly had seven rooms on the downstairs surrounding a courtyard with a picnic table and a chair outside. She lived on the upstairs, what was commonly the case in Belize City. The guesthouse sat behind a tall, vacant building of about five stories, and was tucked away from the street noise and riff-raff. One had to walk through a narrow passage-way, through a gate and around the corner to the right, and, voila, you were there.

"Remember me?" John asked.

"Oh, yes, Mae brought you here, but I didn't have anything available at the time," she replied.

"I called and texted you several times after that," John said.

"I know. I was having phone problems."

Whatever, John thought to himself.

"Did you find a place because this room is available for long term if you would like."

"Not at the moment, I'm living in Chetumal."

"Really? My son lives there. I'm from San Pedro, and I'm of three-quarters Mexican descent. That's a wonderful city, Chetumal, and it's so cheap to live there," she said.

"Yeah, I really like it," John said. "But you never know, I could come back and this is where I'd want to be."

"Well, I hope that you do," she said.

"I'd like to stay for at least one night, maybe three. I'll pay you tomorrow and should know by then how many nights I'll need to stay for."

"Okay, it will be thirty-five dollars for one night, thirty per night if you stay for more than one night."

"That's fine," John said. Then came the hard part for him. "I have a little problem, though, with my bank, and well, right now, I just have pesos. I can give you those as collateral until I sort things out with the bank."

"Okay," she said. "I trust you." She didn't ask for the collateral, and John was safe and sound with a nice room with a private bath but no television. He didn't care.

Molly showed John two rooms that were available, and he chose the latter, which was down a short hallway that had two other apartments within and was directly beneath her home upstairs.

"I like this one," John said. Molly left him with a towel and a roll of toilet paper and off she went.

"Thank God," John said out loud to himself. "This could have ended ugly."

As John was getting situated in his room, he checked his front and back pockets and found a five hundred peso bill in his right back pocket. "*I'll be damned,*" John said to himself. "*I was never five hundred pesos short after all. But it's a damn good thing that I thought I was because it's the only currency I have.*"

John had a free night on his hands and figured he could use his debit card or the pesos as currency or collateral, so he decided to go out and have a little fun. It had been a long, stressful day and a few beers at the Latino bar on Orange Street was in order.

It was now just getting dark at about seven o'clock when John left his room and walked down Queen Street to the swing bridge, where he looked out over the sea to his left at the several sail boats that were docked by the bridge, and realized that these last few days were probably the last time he would take in those sights.

He turned right on Orange Street and walked about four and a half blocks to the bar, where he had not been since his early days in

Belize City when he had gone there with Carlos. John walked in and the place was virtually empty, except for a handful of employees, who were all Hispanic, of course. One of them, a lady with dirty blonde hair, caught his eye immediately, as did he to hers. He sat down at the bar and ordered a stout from the lady behind the bar. She immediately came over and sat next to him to his left in a barstool by the front wall and window.

"Hi, I'm Helen. What is your name?"

"Headley, John Headley," John answered.

"I noticed you walk by this afternoon, and I said to myself, 'Wow, where did he come from?'"

"I came from Chetumal on the bus this afternoon. It's a pleasure to meet you. You noticed me, did you?"

"What girl wouldn't have?"

John could think of one, that being Nakyadi, and chuckled to himself.

"Would you like to buy me a drink, and I'll be yours for the night?"

She was dressed in a short skirt with a buttoned-up blouse tied above the belly button. She looked to be in her early forties and was quite appealing with a nice body. Her breasts stood out loosely and obviously from her scant bra.

"Sure, what'll you have?"

"Whiskey and coke."

"That'll be fourteen dollars for the drink and the stout," the lady bartender said to John. John pulled out his debit card, the one that he had doubts of it having any value at the moment, and tried to hand it to her.

"We don't take credit cards," she said.

Oh yeah, I'm in Belize, I should have known that, John thought to himself. He did know that.

Helen intervened at this point and said to the lady bartender, "Let him run a tab, I'm sure he's good for it."

Oh, boy, here we go. What the hell, John thought to himself.

You see, what they do in these Latino bars in Belize is that they have these pretty girls hustle drinks from guys for ten dollars a pop. John figured they got half and the house kept half.

Helen was from Honduras, but had come to Belize City some eleven years prior and had never gone back. She was married there and long since divorced. John played songs from the jukebox at fifty cents per songs from The Doors, the Rolling Stones, and the like. They didn't hear that kind of music there very often.

John played air guitar on her forearm to "*Light my Fire*" by the Doors and "*Wild Horses*" by the Stones. He nailed it. She said that it hurt a few times, but it was good fun.

She flirted with John and kissed him and touched him. He returned the favor.

"Where are you staying for the night?" she asked.

"I'm staying in a room just around the corner off of Queen Street on Barrack Road," John said.

"I'll come over tonight after I get off, and we'll make love," she said. "You know, and do other things," she added as she stuck her index finger in her mouth.

"Okay, that would be nice. How will you get there? It will be late."

She pointed at the security guy standing at the door, a large hombre with big arms.

"He'll drive me there after I call you later and get directions."

"Sounds good," John said.

"Here, write your number on this napkin." And John did.

"Well, I'd like to wait here for you, but I'm a bit tired. It's been a long day."

John figured he had had six or seven stouts, and she had at least that many whiskey and cokes. It was strange though—she seemed perfectly sober.

"You've got to settle the tab first, though, sweetie," she said.

It was after ten o'clock there, which made it past midnight on the east coast, so John figured he had a shot at a new day's limit on the card.

"I'll need to go down to where the banks are," John said

"Okay, he'll drive us there," she said as she pointed to the big guy.

Helen and John got into the backseat of what appeared to be a fairly nice American-made car, but he wasn't thinking about that at the time.

John got out and went into the ATM room at the Heritage Bank while the two of them waited in the car. John put his card into the machine fearing the worst, and he got just that.

"Your card has expired" was the message on the screen, and the machine spit the card back at him. *Damn, I'm screwed*, John thought as he walked to the street to get into the car.

"It didn't work. I'm having some kind of problem with my bank, and I'll have to sort it out with them on Monday," John told them. He didn't know if the big guy spoke any English or not. He had not and did not say a word.

"All right," Helen said, "I trust you, but we're going to have to hold your passport until then."

"Okay," John said, as they drove back to the bar.

They all got out of the car and went back into the bar, where John said to Helen, "I'm going to walk on back to my room. I'll wait on your call."

John made it back all right, knowing that he shouldn't be walking those streets that late at night. He was just relieved he had gotten back safe and sound and without a broken face from that big guy at the bar, who never said a word.

John was awakened by a phone call at about two o'clock. He didn't answer. *She was half of my problem*, John thought to himself. *I was the other half.* He rolled over and went back to sleep to fight on another day.

John woke up really early, as he always did when he was in a crisis. He was in a crisis.

The banks are closed tomorrow, so I can't convert the pesos, he thought. *What the hell am I going to do?* John had about two dollars and eighty cents in Belizean, credit on his cell phone, and that was it. He called Elisa first and got her voicemail. "Elisa, it's Dad. Please call me ASAP. I've got a crisis." He then tried her mom, Jean, who he knew was there in Stuart with her mother to celebrate the Fourth of July with Elisa. He got her voicemail. "Jean, it's John. Please call me at this number ASAP. I've got a crisis."

John waited impatiently for a couple of hours and heard nothing from either of them. He decided to call Christopher, although he hated doing it since Christopher had been so kind as to send him the brand-new laptop that waited precariously for its new owner. He got his voicemail. "Christopher, it's John. Please call me ASAP. I've got a crisis."

About ten minutes later, John's phone rang. It was Christopher. John told him about his dilemma, hoping that he would have some sympathy for his predicament.

"John, I would help you if I could. I'm in England and am on my way to the Middle East. The family and I are on holiday." That's what they called it in New England and in Europe, *holiday*. Where John came from, they called it vacation.

"Damn, well, I guess I'll have to keep trying Elisa and Jean. I think they're at the beach today. Enjoy your holiday and be safe," John said to Christopher as they said goodbye.

Oh, damn, John thought. *What am I going to do?*

Then John thought of George. They hadn't departed on a particularly good note when John had last seen George because John had told him that he might need to stay in his room with him for a night or two while John was thinking that he needed to wait on his computer to arrive before leaving for Chetumal. For some stupid reason, George decided to tell Nelly that that might be the case, and she told him that "Frank didn't want Molly in that room." John knew that that was a big lie; Nelly didn't want John in George's room. She wanted to make life as difficult as possible for John. So John kind of, sort of, yelled at George and said, "Why the hell did you do that? Why did you tell Nelly? That's none of her business. Did you tell Nelly before you brought home all of those stray felines? I didn't think so."

Well, George didn't take too kindly to that tongue lashing, so he said, "Watch out, son, or I'm going to take you down." Those had been the last words spoken between them.

But it was looking more and more like George would be John's only hope—truly his last resort. And it wasn't as though John and George hadn't had previous falling outs. One night when he, George and Zulme, were in George's room drinking beer, John got mad at George for being too nice to Nelly. After all, George knew what she had done to John, and it irritated him that George didn't seem to let that get in the way of his friendly relationship with her.

"Why the hell are such good buddies with that bitch?" John asked.

George then jumped from his bed, while John and Zulme were on the other one, and said, "Son, I haven't been taken down by too many men, and you aren't going to be one who does."

Zulme got very upset with George after having witnesses such a potentially violent tirade and called for a cab to go home, which she did. The next morning, George popped his head in John's room and asked, "Would like me to fry you some eggs?"

John knew that George had a short memory, and he was, generally speaking, a really good guy.

John decided to take the short walk over to Mae's house on the off chance that George would be there. He had spent his last dollar on a coke earlier that morning and literally had zero money other than pesos, nor did he have any food.

At this point, John's heart was racing. He approached the house, and it seemed quiet and empty inside. *Not a good sign*, John thought to himself as he approached the front gate. He walked up to the window by the side front door and called inside, "George, hey, George, are you in there?"

"Well, it sure as hell ain't Aunt Bee," George retorted from inside the cinderblock, three-room house, in his usual humorous fashion. "Come on in, John. How the hell are you and what the hell are you doing back here in Belize City?" George asked.

"I had to come back to pick up my new laptop, you remember, right?"

"Sure as hell do, that's a good thing," George said. "Where are you staying?"

"I'm staying over there at Molly's guesthouse, remember, the one that I liked that had that really nice patio tucked away down that little walkway and to the right."

"Really? Hell, yes, I remember. That's good."

"Well," John said. "I have a bit of a problem. You see, I got here with no Belizean dollars only a bunch of pesos and my ATM card won't work, that's a long story, and well, I don't have any money."

"Well, you came to the right place at the right time," George said. "I just got back from the bank. My annuity payment came in early. I got lucky. How much do you need?"

John's heart and stomach surged with relief and gratitude. George was truly his savior at that moment on that given day.

"Well, let's see, I need about one hundred and twenty five dollars to make it through until Monday when the banks back in the States are open," John said.

"Not a problem," George said.

"I'll give you that equivalency in pesos. Let me see, yeah, that's about one thousand pesos, here," as John handed him the money.

"Thank God for you, George, thank you very much."

"No problem. I'm just glad I could help." And that was truly the case. George had a big heart.

"I haven't eaten all day," John said, "so I'm going to run over to that Chinese restaurant and get something to eat and then I'll come back to see you and Mae this afternoon. Where is Mae, by the way?"

"Her ex was shot and killed a night or two ago. She's dealing with that, you know, funeral arrangements and the like."

"Shot and killed by who? And for what?"

"Had to do with drugs, I don't know who did it. I'm staying away from that one."

"Can't say that I blame you on that one, George," John said as he got up to leave. "Great to see you again."

"Great to see you too, John," George replied.

John had rarely been so relieved and thankful in his life. He walked to the Chinese restaurant with a totally new outlook and a bounce of confidence and elation in his stride. He later went to the internet café and got into his email for the first time in two weeks. There were the usual junk mails and dozens and dozens of messages from women in the Philippines. That was a whole other story for another day. There was also an e-mail from his publisher asking for an address to have his ten copies of his book shipped to.

That evening, John bought five of his beloved Belikin stouts and sat in his room that night, drinking them and relaxing after a rigorous and prolonged case of the heebie-jeebies. He would never get a call from his own daughter or her mother, his ex-wife.

The next morning, John awakened with a renewed spirit, confident that he could pull off the rest of his trip. His door was open, and a young, very pretty black girl popped her head around the corner of the door and said to John, "Would you like a cup of coffee?"

"Sure, that would be great. I love coffee. My name's John. What's yours?" John asked.

"I'm Daisy," she said. "I live across the hall." John knew that because the day before, he had seen her lying on the couch watching TV with her door open. She was so hot. She was wearing a silk buttoned-up shirt with shirttails and only her panties underneath. John knew that because when they stepped across the hall and into her apartment, she sat down on the couch, and John could see straight to her panties, nothing else in between.

"Yeah, I saw you there yesterday," John said, as he followed her into her apartment.

"I saw you too," she said.

She placed the water in the pot on the stove and lit it. She then handed John a large, nice ceramic coffee cup and said, "Here's the milk and sugar."

"Where's your cup?" John asked.

"Oh, I don't like coffee," she said.

That's kind of odd. Inviting a complete and utter stranger into her apartment for coffee when she doesn't even drink it, John thought to himself as the water was coming to a boil. "Really? Then what are you going to drink?" John asked her.

"Oh, nothing, I'm fine," she said.

John made his coffee, and she said, "Come and have a seat. So, tell me, have you moved here, are you moving here?" Daisy asked.

Damn, now I might wish that I had or did or might? John thought to himself. "No, I don't think so. I was trying to about a month ago, but Molly told me that she was full at the time, even though she wanted the girl who was in my room to be out of it."

"Oh, you're the guy that she mentioned to me. I see now. Where are you living now and how long are you staying here?"

"I'm just here for a few days, then I'm headed back to Chetumal, where I recently rented an apartment."

"Oh, I like Chetumal. We used to go partying over there, to the clubs, you know. Would you like another cup of coffee?" Daisy asked.

"Yes, maybe a half cup, I'd like that," John answered back.

John heard a young girl cry from the bedroom.

"That's my little girl," Daisy said. "She probably wants something to drink."

Daisy got up and opened the door to the bedroom, and there was the cutest little one-year-old sitting up in bed, her hair was jet black, and it was curly and thick, and she had big bright eyes. She stared a moment at John, as if to gauge the circumstances, and then smiled. John smiled back and said hello. Daisy went in and laid down on the bed with her and put a bottle of juice in her daughter's hands. Daisy's legs were bent at the knees as she lay on her side, and as she rolled onto her back after giving the little darling her bottle, John could see Daisy's panties clearly—white cotton ones with little pink and baby blue flowers on them. He couldn't help but become aroused. And he knew that she knew that she was showing herself to him, inviting him to indulge in her.

Daisy was about five feet and three inches and had smooth and silky light-brown skin. Her hair was cut at the bottom of her neck, and she had a very pretty and feminine face. Her breasts were firm and a light creamy brown and of medium size—a perfect size. Her body was fantastic. *I wonder why she invited me over for coffee?* John asked himself. *She doesn't even drink coffee. And dressed like that? And I know there's a man involved here, and it's not just me.*

"What do you do?" Daisy asked, "I mean, for a living."

"Nothing much," John said. "I just wrote a book that's coming out this summer."

"Really, how cool," Daisy said. "What's it called? What's it about?"

"It's called *On Both Sides of the Street*, and it's about my life, only all the names are different. You know, in third person."

"Oh, okay, I see. Where are you from?"

"The States, Atlanta," John replied. "And you? Where are you from?"

"Dangriga," Daisy said.

Then Daisy started telling John her life story, really personal stuff. About the little girl's father, who was Hispanic and Belizean. She told John that they had had an up-and-down relationship, mostly down. She said that he beat her many times, but now when he was around and did that, she fought back. She was clearly trapped in a situation she desperately wanted a way out of. John thought that she thought that that might be him. And all in a half-hour. Amazing.

"*Says she is going to go. You better not run and you better not hide. You better love loving and you better behave. Woman in chains. Woman in chains. Trades her soul as skin and bones. Sells the only thing she owns. Well I feel deep in your soul there are wounds time can't heal. And I feel like somebody somewhere is trying to breath. And it's a world gone crazy. Woman in chains. The sun and the moon. The wind and the rain. Woman in chains. So free. So free.*"

"How old are you?" Daisy asked John. "Thirty-something?"

Damn, John thought. *Why do all these women always ask me how old I am? I feel like I'm auditioning for something.* He probably was, in their eyes and minds.

"No, I'm older than that," John said. *Damn, sweet girl, Dwight Eisenhower was president when I was born. I think, anyway, I don't even remember, it was so long ago. I'm older than most dirt*, John was thinking to himself, wondering how things had come to pass as they were at that moment. He could have been her grandfather, chronologically speaking.

"And how old are you?"

"Twenty-four."

"You're a baby, a pretty one at that," John said.

"Thank you. I wish you were moving in here. I like your company. I like being around you," she said.

Daisy did the same thing the following morning, appearing before John's door at about nine o'clock. "Come and have some coffee with me, okay?"

"Sure, Daisy, thank you very much. You know I love coffee," he said, as John gnawed on his knuckles in an attempt to contain his desire for her. You know, a kind of displaced oral fixation of sorts. John was thinking that he could love her very easily.

She told him about her job at the Celebrity restaurant, the nicest in town, only a few blocks away on the road directly by the sea. She said that she worked six days a week, some with split shifts, like Saturday and Sunday, and that she only made four hundred dollars biweekly. She was an assistant cook to the chef and was an apprentice. She couldn't afford a phone, and her mostly estranged boyfriend and father to her daughter didn't help much.

John felt awful for her. Her eyes were screaming out for help. "Please take me away, please be my knight in shining armor." He knew that if he had wanted to, he could have swept her away from her awful circumstance and taken good care of her, but that wouldn't be right or fair to either of them in the long run, especially her. A part of John felt that he could fall in love with her so easily.

And John knew that she was attracted to him and liked him very much; it was what she clearly wanted. He, this man on the outer edges of middle age, and she, a beautiful and naïve girl with her whole life ahead of her with her new daughter? No, that wouldn't be right. Life has its normal progression and that would not be normal. She was the sweetest, welcoming, and enticing girl he had met in a very long time, but she was a child, a world away from John's world. John would be sad when he had to say goodbye to her.

Later that morning, Daisy had to get ready for work, and John was sitting out on the patio reading his Spanish translation book and dictionary. He had bought it at the Plaza de la Americas a couple of weeks before. And then it dawned on him—it was the most awful of feelings—that tomorrow was the Fourth of July and all the banks, namely his, would be closed. He was almost out of money and still needed to pay for the room for one more night and just live through until Tuesday morning, when he knew he would be able to remedy the situation with his bank. He decided he would go to the well once more, and that well, well, would be George.

He decided to walk over to Mae's house to see him and ask him if he could convert, still yet, some more pesos. John walked to her house, and George was there, but no one else. They were moving the next day to a new apartment in King's Park, and Mae was out shopping.

John hollered through the window, and George said to come on in. "What's going on?" George asked.

"Nothing much, just trying to get ready for a big day on Tuesday, and I have yet another problem," John said.

"Well, what is it?" George asked.

"The banks are closed in the States tomorrow, and well, you guessed it, I'm out of money again," John said.

"Well, you're in luck, because Mae's not here to watch over me, and I have a secret stash of money. How much do you need?"

"I'd say about thirty-five dollars," John said.

"Let me see what I can do for you," George said as he got up and went into their bedroom. He came back out and said, "Here's fifty, and don't give me any pesos for it. It's yours, here, take it."

"You're a godsend, George, I don't know how to thank you enough."

"By taking it, that's how," George said.

They exchanged pleasantries about George and Mae's new apartment and how good things were going in Chetumal for John.

John said goodbye to George, and that probably would be the last time he would ever see him again. What a kind and generous man, this man named George, was.

John awoke on the Fourth of July excited and energized for what lay ahead the next day. He had his usual cup of coffee with Daisy, and they got to know one another a bit more. She was adorable, as usual. She deserved more from life, and when he was with her, he wanted to make love to her every second of their conversations and interactions but resisted any attempt at doing so—at that moment, that is. Daisy was working a double shift that afternoon and night, so he wouldn't see her until the next morning.

Later that morning, John decided to take a walk to the tourist village, which he had never been to before, and then walk out to the end of the peninsula where the river feeds the sea and converts to a salty base as its once-distant cousin, the sea, was. The village was comprised of various eateries and coffee shops, souvenir shops, and vendors of travel excursions.

At the southeastern-most tip of the peninsula stood the Radisson Hotel. John didn't go inside because he had no money to spend and couldn't see the point otherwise. He had stayed in many, many more luxurious hotels.

John then went to the internet café, where he hoped that he would find that goddess of a woman he had seen that past Friday, but she wasn't there. He then decided to go to the Bank of Belize and convert some more pesos, though he didn't think he would need them now.

On his walk there, just on the other side of the swing bridge, John ran into none other than Carlos, who at eight-thirty in the morning, had a beer in his hand.

"Where have you been, John? Where did you go?" Carlos asked.

"I moved to Chetumal," John replied.

"Really? What are you doing here?"

"I came back to town to pick up a new laptop computer. What are you doing here drinking beer at this time of the morning?"

"I've got a small job down the street doing some sheet rock. Maria left me, she'd had enough, I guess."

"Where did she and Fatima go?"

"I don't know, somewhere here in Belize City."

"Well, it's probably for the best. You'd look at her in ten years and say to yourself, what the hell am I doing? What was I thinking?"

"Well, I'm trying to get over it. I guess that's why I'm drinking this beer." John thought that was kind of funny since Carlos had either a beer or rum in his hands every waking hour that his budget would allow.

"Well, I'm going to the bank to exchange some pesos for some dollars. I guess I'll see you on down the road," John said, as they went their separate ways for the last time.

He went to the same lady as he had that prior Friday, which seemed so long ago to John, somehow. Oddly enough, she said they didn't convert pesos into dollars, only the US dollar, the Canadian dollar and the British pound. No rubles, and no pesos. And Mexico was their neighbor, what a shame. John didn't really care.

John then went to the park that stood between the bank and Brodie's department store and the courthouse directly across the street to the east. He went there to see his old friend Rico, who had been John's supplier of black market cigarettes. Rico was there, as he most always was, and he bought a couple of packs for five dollars and told Rico that he had moved to Mexico and that he came to bid him farewell.

The next morning, John awoke with one more very important task to take care of, and a potentially daunting task, and that was to call his bank and get his card reactivated. He had only about two dollars left on his phone, and they moved and talked at a pretty leisurely pace up there in central Georgia.

The first time he tried, just after seven o'clock, what was nine o'clock there, a man answered the phone saying, "Hello," instead of, "F & M Bank, may I help you?"

What a dumbass, John thought, so he hung to try again in a few minutes and in hopes that a non-moron would answer.

John was in luck, and he was promptly transferred to Rhonda upstairs. She knew John from his many travails with his card over the past two years. She quickly activated the card and apologized for the trouble. John was all set now.

He went to the bank and withdrew four hundred and fifty dollars, which amount he thought would be sufficient to cover the laptop, the Latino bar tab (*You dumbass, you,* John thought to himself) and for a little food and the bus fare of twelve dollars to Chetumal.

The money was successfully dispensed from the machine. "What a great damn, fucking relief," John said to himself as he quickly headed for the post office. The package was there as promised, the money tendered, and off John went to open the box with Daisy. She was excited, and it was a beautiful thing to behold, both the computer and her.

John told her that he was leaving later that morning for Chetumal, and she seemed shocked and disappointed.

"You are leaving? Today?" she said with a sadness in her eyes. "Yes, but who knows, Daisy, I might be back, and if I do come back, I will come and find you," John said.

"That would be nice," she said.

They exchanged Facebook addresses, and he gave her a kiss goodbye. "If you ever need to get away for a few days, write to me and tell me. I would love for you to come, both literally and figuratively," John said. He guessed that she probably didn't quite get that but probably later would. He could envision her sitting on the couch thinking about him and what his last words were, and then having that Leslie Nielsen look from the movie, *The Naked Gun,* where Priscilla Presley looks into his freezer, and there's a carton of Chinese food in there, and she says to him, "Joe Gong's restaurant? They closed years ago," and Leslie looks into the camera, and he has that look of "Really? Whoops." Daisy then probably said to herself with a grin, something like "That bad, bad boy."

And then John left.

John's new laptop was now safely in his backpack as he left Molly's quaint little guesthouse as he headed for the dreaded bar on

Orange Street to pay the tab and get his passport. Most essential it was, that passport.

John negotiated the swing bridge and then Orange Street for the last time. He got to the bar at about ten-thirty, leaving an hour until the bus for Chetumal would set sail.

The lady behind the bar, a different one, said, "That'll be one hundred and fifty dollars."

"That's not right," John said. "I counted the drinks, and she had six or seven and I had six stouts."

"The tab says she had twelve drinks," the bitch said.

"The tab's wrong. You've stuffed the tab, and you know it. I have a relationship with the Belize Tourism Board, and they'll hear about this," John said. "Where's my passport?"

The bitch reached under the counter, and John looked at and said, "You know this isn't right, bitch," as he paid her the money and quickly left.

Passport now in hand, John proceeded briskly around the corner by the bus station, past the smelly Conch Bay fish market and over and across the Bell China Bridge and the Belize River below, and then on to the intersection of Freetown Road. As he was walking, he wondered how many miles he had walked around the city of Belize since moving there.

"Let's see, I lived here about nine hundred days and probably averaged about two miles per day. I'll be damned, I bet I walked one thousand eight hundred miles while I lived here, and all that walking was done in flip-flops. Amazing." He was then on Baymen Avenue, headed north, and there on the left was GS-Com, where inside his deceased computer lay in wait for the donor transplant. It was then about eleven o'clock.

"Hi, Erika. This adventure with my laptop is about to end," he said, as he pulled the shiny new laptop from his backpack.

"Yeah, I know, right?" she said. She was very pretty too, but John didn't have any time to dwell on or deal with that aspect of the situation. She had a bit of eastern Indian in her and was from Orange Walk, as was Carla.

She called one of the technicians upstairs, and a guy quickly came down and got his new laptop and went back upstairs. They knew the drill; Emir had briefed them. The long-awaited transplant was about to begin. "Is the deceased's donor information in order? Yes, okay, then we shall proceed."

"I'm trying to catch the eleven-thirty bus to Chetumal, so please be as quick as you can," John said to Erika, who then picked up the phone and relayed the message.

He came back downstairs with his new and old laptop, transplant complete. It's amazing what one hundred and eighty six thousand miles per second can do to expedite matters. Erika said, "That'll be forty-five dollars." To John, that was a damn good deal as he had spent many times on the phone with Emir, the lead technician, who happened to be on vacation that week. John paid it with his bank card and placed the new recipient of said transplant into the backpack. "You can keep the old one," John said. "Maybe you can make use of some of its organs." He laughed and said goodbye to Erika, the pretty one from Orange Walk.

It was eleven-fifteen, and everything had gone exactly as planned. He arrived at the bus station with five minutes to spare, which was time to smoke a cigarette and take a breather (that probably sounds incongruent) before boarding the bus.

John boarded the bus, and his mission and adventure to Belize City had been done. It had been a complete and utter success. John's final chapter about Belize City had been written; the book was closed for good.

As the bus slowly moved northward and to the bridge, where they would turn north, and slowly navigate the roundabout and head northwest, he said goodbye to Belize City. Even a horrible existence there had provided some fond memories that John would never forget.

They crossed over the final bridge out of town and through Ladyville, and then on the pretty much nothing until they would arrive in Orange Walk in about an hour and a half.

John was relieved and started thinking about the bizarre trip and Helen and Daisy, and then he started thinking about other interludes with women and with girls that he had had through the years and how each meant nothing but left a mark, a memory, nonetheless.

If nothing else, these encounters were bizarre, to say the least. One of John's first memories of such a triste happened when he was working in Jacksonville, straight out of college and still dating Leila back in Knoxville. He drove up in June for his first vacation in his new life in the professional world to see her and all his friends, who were mostly still there in Knoxville, just trying to figure out a way to prolong their college life of debauchery.

John remembered that he and Leila and her roommate, Janet, had gone out to a bar to listen to ole Wild Bill Hickok, a one-man show of a band at one of the local bars down on the so-called strip or Cumberland Avenue. He played everything—the guitar, the drums, the bass, and the harmonica, and sang and was one of the local favorites. Janet's little sister was visiting from King's Port and was a senior at the local high school in King's Port, the same one John had attended and still the only high school in King's Port. Some others were there with John and Leila, Janet, and her little sister, but John just couldn't remember who—it was from a time so long ago.

Well, Janet's little sister, who was only seventeen but very hot, and I mean a woman in full, took a liking to John. He couldn't remember for the life of him what her name had been, or still was, for that matter. They gazed into each other's eyes as the beer and music flowed, as in a love song. As to John, oblivious to his lover and girlfriend, Leila, and as to Janet's sister (what was her name anyway?), oblivious to her observant and infuriated big sister.

They worked their way around the mass of people to each other, eyes locked and then fingers and bodies touched. It was like out of some kind of love story of the past, you know, like Romeo and Juliet, but they weren't thinking of that. They must have been highly buzzed, and yes, drunk, because the two of them left the bar together and went back to John's old house by the park a block away, leaving Leila and the rest of them behind at the bar and proceeded to get in bed, a bed that now was somebody else's bed, as John had moved out six months earlier.

John didn't know, or care, whose it was the upstairs bedroom that he had lived in with Mark. Anyway, nobody else is at the house, so anyway, she's on top of John and they're making love, and I mean they're really going at it, like she was some kind of rodeo star or something, and her older sister, Janet, comes barging into the room and yells to her sister, "Get off of him!" Whoops, certainly one of life's more embarrassing moments, at least for this particular non-gentleman who went by the name of John Headley.

"This is Captain Kirk of the USS *Enterprise*. Yeah, and I'm here with Spock, and we've got a problem, or at least Spock does. Beam me up, Scottie."

John and Janet, and for that matter, Leila, didn't get along very well with each other after that episode. John and Janet never spoke to one another again, and that was probably the beginning of the end for him and Leila, although she was one of the sweetest of girls he had ever met. He probably should have married her, and everything would have been all right.

Years later, in downtown Atlanta, when John was working for Solar Life and really getting serious about his career, he was up on the executive suite floor, one above his, making copies of some voluminous document because they, the legal department, had the most capable of printers in the company. A pretty young paralegal named Jennifer was in the copier room too, which was adjacent to the legal offices, and they had a brief conversation, one of their first few conversations ever. She was wearing, as John so vaguely recalled, a bluish-gray skirt with a cream white blouse, her body gushing in its youth and lustful yearning. She said to John, "I can't believe I'm about to say this to you, but I'd really like to have your baby."

John tried thinking to himself what had just confronted him. This from a young, hot recent college graduate, of whom he had just a casual, work relationship with, and worked right there alongside John and the rest of the accounting department downstairs. *"How could she risk it all by being so brazen and oblivious to corporate eti-*

quette? Is she just trying to 'climb the corporate ladder,' or is she just really horny?" John asked himself, always one step ahead of his potential pursuers.

To which, alas, John said the only thing plausible in that situation and at that particular point in time, "Really? When would you like to start that process?"

"Right now," she said, as she closed the door shut behind her, copier a-blazing and no one else in sight to be seen or to be heard from.

And there was that time in Scottsdale. John was there at a special risk reinsurance conference hosted by a brokerage firm out of Toronto for their reinsurer clients. It was the night after they had had that marvelous hot air balloon jaunt over the desert north of Scottsdale and landed in the middle of the desert and had a steak dinner with red wine around a big campfire, while the sun set and night began closing in.

The following night, they, a group of some thirty or so people, had dinner and an open bar at the resort. There was one particular lady there, from a firm out of Toronto, who John began to strike up a conversation with. He remembered her from the previous client gathering down in Fort Lauderdale the year before, where she had clearly let her attraction to John become apparent. She was pretty with dark, curly hair set on her shoulders and piercing blue eyes and snow- white skin but with a husband back in Toronto, which she made clear early on. John always saw those defenses as Trojan horses, with an attack imminent on the horizon.

After several drinks and the party winding down, John and her, he couldn't for the life of him remember her name, wound up naked in the hot tub by the pool. They then proceeded to his room and got into bed. He'll never forget her saying, "My, you have a very nice d—."

To which, John replied, "Thank you. Yes, he's very, very nice. I take him with me wherever I go. He's usually asleep but can sometimes be the life of the party."

And then there was one evening in early spring when John was living at Lake Oconee. This was shortly after he was beat down and suffered at the hands of the policeman in Athens, so John was in an arm sling and a wrist and thumb brace. He was walking to his car to go and get some beer that early evening, and a pretty young girl with brown hair—that's all he could tell from that distance—waved at him from across the parking lot. John waved back and, thinking nothing of it, got into his car and stopped on his way out of the complex to rid himself of some trash across from the pool. As he proceeded up the long hill to the exit, the same girl was walking along the way. John stopped and asked her if she needed a ride, to which she replied, "That would be great."

Well, as it turned out, she was walking to the market next to the McDonald's to do the same, so John went inside and bought two six-packs for the two of them. They went back to her apartment, where she had just moved in with her grandmother, who was apparently asleep in her bedroom.

They sat on her patio, enjoying the evening of a new spring, talking about what had brought them to the crossroads in that they now found themselves. She had fled South Carolina and the physical abuse and control of her boyfriend and had enrolled at the university in Milledgeville. John wasn't sure what had brought him to this place in life and just said he was waiting for the right time to move back to Atlanta.

She—John couldn't, for the life of him, remember her name—moved her chair closer to John and put her arm around him and kissed him on the cheek. The next thing he knew, a six-pack later a piece, they were on the couch, butt naked, making love.

Afterward, she said to John, "Wow, I don't know what got into me, I don't normally do things like that." To which, John replied, "Really? I do."

What do all these encounters of a single and simple moment have in common, you might ask? Nothing really, just a brief encounter with a person that they would never see again, but in each of their lives, a moment that they would likely never forget and likely taught them something about themselves, be it good, bad, or indifferent. That they were, when all is said and done, just human, and humans do seemingly uncharacteristic things sometimes.

And just a couple of weeks later, John was at the Silver Moon bar on an early Friday night, and the place was jammed packed. John was sitting at the bar, which was on the right side of the place, and the restaurant was on the left, with the bathrooms directly in the center beyond the vestibule of entry. John got up from his place at the bar and walked through the standing-room only crowd to try to get at the men's room. There were three young ladies standing by its door, each with a beer in hand, and when John was about to enter, one of them said to John, "Can we come in and hold it for you?"

John smiled at the three pretty ladies, one at a time, and then said, "There's only room for two hands, so I'm afraid one of you will have to sit this one out. You can decide among yourselves, or we can draw straws." To that, the ladies laughed hysterically.

It was a harmless and funny encounter, but one that I bet they would never forget. I can just hear the girl who had initiated the conversation telling someone else later, John thought, laughing to himself. *And can you believe I said that? I mean, it's just so unlike me, right? I'd never seen that guy before. I don't know what got into me.*

Humored by his memories and content with his soon-to-be new home, John looked out at the large nothingness of the north central landscape of Belize as the bus rolled along.

Viva, Mexico!

N ow back at his new apartment and largely unscathed from his trip back to Belize City, John reflected on his newfound luck, if you will. *Everything seems to be going right*, John thought to himself as he sat at his kitchen table in the heat of the middle day. *Even when I inject myself into situations and seemingly try to get in the way of myself, I seem to always, lately, that is, come out like a charmed sojourner. I escaped Belize City when it could have been a very, very bad ending. In Belize, everything sucked and everything usually went wrong.*

There, John's pervasive feeling was: *"If the Bible's right, the world's going to explode. I've been trying to get as far away from myself as I can."*

"I lost my essential laptop computer, and now look at what I have. I've met and had many women much younger than me, while many men my age just hope that they can keep their wives of thirty-some odd years. The cyst, which suddenly and mysteriously emerged a couple of inches from my left armpit and that has haunted me for four or five years now, just up and decided to pop itself a couple of weeks ago when I had been scheduled for minor surgery by Dr. Guitterez back in June and skipped out on it to come to Chetumal. And the blockage around my right ear drum, which happened about every five years or so, and had happened again in May and was congenital in its origin, just went away. I normally had to go see an internal medicine doctor to have the junk sucked out. And then there's my new apartment. I have space, and I have peace and quiet, and I now have six chairs in total. Four around the kitchen table and two in my bedroom. I had no chair in my room in Belize City, only a bed. And then I met Olga, a true godsend of a person to me."

But John's inner self told him, *"John, things aren't always as bad as they might seem, and conversely, things aren't as good as they might seem. Keep an even keel, and you'll be the better for it."*

Carla, too, was in John's life more and more as each day passed. They waved to each other in the morning as she opened at about seven-thirty, just after John had taken his shower after a workout and some coffee. It was something they had to do to start their respective days, to validate the other's importance in their lives. They knew when to look over at each other and give little gestures, without having spoken about them. John left her notes on her desk at the front of the salon, and when she would see him later, she would say, "I have all your notes, right here in my iPhone case. See?" There was certainly a lot going on with their relationship, and John didn't quite know what to make of it.

There was something mysterious about it, and John was all but convinced that she had a boyfriend, but not in Orange Walk but right there in Chetumal. She hadn't shown up that previous Sunday night, and sometimes she seemed nervous that people might be watching them as they talked and touched on the street. And she hadn't bothered introducing him to her father, which is always probably not a very good sign. Something was just not right.

He would stop by her salon later in the morning after he had checked his e-mails at Olga's, and they spoke briefly of the evening ahead and kissed goodbye as another long day in Chetumal was beginning. They looked forward to that night, as always, when they would share time together as they most always did, each and every night. She had told John that she loved him and that she wanted to be Carla Headley. Between you and me, John didn't think he needed another newly minted Headley walking down the aisle of a church and by his side. He was far too old for that and had, well, been there and done that twice—perhaps, more than he should have. That just wasn't going to happen. In life, you play with the cards that you're dealt, and that just wasn't in the cards John held.

Olga kept telling John, "I don't know Carla, but watch out. Take your time. You can have any woman you want, that is, that's not married." And then she stopped in her breath and said, "Well, sadly, I'm not so sure that's true either. Anyway, I read your writing, and at that, you are a very smart man. Not so much when it comes to women. I try to look out for you, but you don't listen."

John had, in such a short period of time, grown to be a lot fonder of Olga. She was extremely intelligent and held two master's degrees, one in information technology and the other in linguistics. And, man, was she funny. She loved to laugh and more often than not found John to be hilarious, largely in his wit, but more so in his day-to-day, nonphysical clumsiness as he clamored around that Mexican city, desperately trying to communicate with people.

"You're so smart, John, yet I have to look over your shoulder all the time. Why can't you see and take care of the most basic and obvious things in life. All the while, you're thinking of crazy things above and beyond outside of the box, while the rest of us are in the box saying, 'We're in here, John. You're so funny,'" she said. "Watch out, I tell you, women and sex will get you in all kinds of trouble. And they will find you here, trust me. Apparently, a few already have."

"I hear you and appreciate what you say, and I am cautious and I respect what you say to me and what you teach me," John said.

"No, you don't," Olga replied, and then she would laugh in her deeply genuine way that was so appealing.

John could not recall ever having reached such a close friendship in such a short period of time with anyone as he had with Olga. And a woman at that—truly unprecedented in John's lifetime. They knew each other well, although she would always tell John when it came to women, "I don't know you well enough to know what you want. An intellect, a free-thinker, a rich woman, a poor woman, a bimbo with a gorgeous body and no brains, and I think, yes, just that, but I just don't know you well enough."

John would laugh and say, "Yes, you do, Olga, yes, you do, you little devil, you. You know me well and I'm an open book for you to read."

"Trust me, John, they will swoop down upon you and suck your blood away. I know, I've seen it happen, time and time again. Don't let that happen to you. The girl in the high heels and short skirt that was over here with my dentist friend while you were staying here, she's not for you. I talked to her, and she's not very smart. Not a lot going on upstairs."

"But she's so hot," John said.

"You and you're 'she's so hot' stuff. Get over it and find a woman with a brain and some morals. There's more to a woman than sex," she said.

"Really? I didn't know that, obviously," John said. Olga was a funny and insightful woman, and she was where John always turned when he needed help, advice as just a friend.

Later that night, while John was waiting to go and visit with Carla, he was sitting out on the veranda and enjoying a beer and the sights and sounds of the street, and he noticed a disturbing sequence of events. A man was standing on the front step—there was only one step—of the Estetica Carla talking to Carla, who faced John from the front of her salon. There were a lot of arm gestures going on with him, and he was clearly agitated by something. Then another man emerged from the left of the salon on the sidewalk, and it appeared the two men were actually, somehow, all in shocking silence to John as he looked on, confronting her about something. Something that John was all but sure was about him. They looked to be in their late twenties or early thirties and appeared to be Latino.

After about fifteen minutes, the newcomer on the left walked away, leaving just the man in front with his foot and leg perched on her entryway. Occasionally, he motioned with his arms up and down, flailing away at something in thought, an issue which didn't appear to be pleasant.

Then John saw the man try to grab her by the right arm, and Carla shook herself free, pushing his arm away violently and stormed into the back of the salon and out of view from John. The man turned and walked away to the left as the other man had done several minutes before. *This doesn't look good*, John thought to himself, as he was now sure that this was her boyfriend and that John's relationship with her was at the crux of the matter. The last thing John wanted at this point, or at any point for that matter, was to be shipped back to the States in a body bag.

This isn't my deal, not my cross to bear, John thought to himself as he tried to digest what had just transpired. It was then about nine-thirty, and John waited to see if Carla would reappear. She did, sweeping the front area where the three of them had stood.

Should I go and see her, just as planned? John wondered. *Or should I just call it a night and consult with Olga tomorrow?* He should have chosen the latter, but instead, John went down the steps and across the avenue to confront her.

"I just saw what happened here," John said.

"What? What just happened here?" Carla responded.

"You know what I'm talking about. I just saw it happen. Is it safe to be here? Should I come over? Do you still want me to come over?" John asked.

"That's a question for you, not me," Carla said.

"What? A question for me? No, it's a question for you. Do you want me here or not, now, right now?"

"That's up to you."

"You just told me you loved me today. You've told me that you want to live with me."

"That? That wasn't serious. I didn't really mean that."

"Really? I'm confused," John said, as he turned away and walked back across the avenue to his apartment.

Then safe and sound back at his apartment, John was dazed and confused. But really, he realized, there shouldn't be any confusion here at all. It was all too clear what had happened and that he was a third rail in this triangle of passion that couldn't turn out well for him. *What should I do?* John wondered.

John slept on that question and went to see Olga the next morning. He told her all about the episode from the night before. She wasn't surprised.

"Were the men Belizean or Mexican?" Olga asked.

"I don't know. How does a person tell the difference?" John answered.

"Well, if there were two of them, they were probably Belizean. Mexican people handle personal matters one on one. Oh my god. I told you, John, you're going to get hurt."

"No, I'm not, that's silly," John said.

"You're something else altogether, John," Olga said.

John and Olga then watched music videos on YouTube of the Rolling Stones and Dire Straits. Olga loved them all and said she had never heard of Dire Straits.

"They don't come around here, I don't think," she said. She then said that Mick was a sexy man. John thought he was awesome as well but didn't see that in him.

Olga told John that her husband from Haiti was coming the next day. His name was Alain. "What a coincidence," John said.

"Why did you leave Haiti?"

"The physical abuse had gotten to be too much to take," she said.

"Really?" John said. "That's awful, I'm so sorry."

Later that afternoon, John was heading out for a couple of tacos when he, for the second time that week, shut the door to his apartment and realized that he had locked himself out. *What a dumb ass I am*, John thought to himself. He had done the same thing on Tuesday and had to go to Olga, who, of course, knew a technician to call, and he soon came and remedied the situation for one hundred and twenty pesos.

John's subliminal instinct was to run to the women in life, whichever one was closer at the time, Olga or Carla. Carla happened to be out in front of Estetica Carla, sweeping the walkway. He walked across the avenue and told her what he had done.

"John, really? Again? I don't know what I'm going to do with you. You'll have to go and tell Olga so that she can call the same guy who got you in a few days ago." She didn't say a word about the previous night or anything, which John found refreshing. She just said, "You're a *booboo*. Come and see me later tonight, please. I want to talk to you. My family in Belize want to meet you."

John walked down the street to the east and the next block and the street of Venustiano Carranza, which he had done several times a day since moving into his apartment.

John told Olga what he had done, and she just laughed. "John, you're a *booboo*."

She called her connection and the same *hombre* came on his motorcycle and tool chest and just laughed at the sight of John. He opened the door in a flash and charged John a measly eighty pesos. John was clearly a *booboo*, but life was good. He would see Carla later that night, and she didn't mention anything of the night before, nor did John.

John met Alain that following Sunday, and a wonderful man he was. Alain was about the same size and build as John and probably about the same age. He had a full gray beard and wore glasses. He spoke French, Spanish, and some English. He was a civil engineer working on a project on the northern coast of Haiti but lived in Port-au-Prince. He and Olga had been apart for over ten years, when she had come to Chetumal with her daughter, Maya, and earned her two master's degrees since and leased her place known as the Posada Inn.

Alain seemed like the most kind and gentle of persons. Shortly after they had met, Alain went back to Olga's and his bedroom and came back with a t-shirt with lettering in French and gave it to John, as a gesture of friendship and validation of the relationship that John and Olga had.

The three of them agreed that they would watch the movie, *A Fish Called Wanda*, later that week, featuring John Cleese, Kevin Kline, and Jamie Lee Curtis. They had never seen or heard of it before, but John considered it to be one of the funniest movies of all time.

Alain had a guitar that he kept there at the inn, and he brought it out one afternoon, having heard from Olga that John had once played the guitar. He took it out of its soft case and handed it to John, who said that he would be glad to tune it for Alain. It was a bit smaller than a normal-size acoustic, which John thought was good if he was going to pick up the craft again. John took the *Española* guitar back to his apartment and tuned it, which surprised John he could still do, and began playing. He quickly remembered the chords and the three-finger pick and roll, and before he knew it, John was playing like he once had, almost.

I guess it's kind of like riding a bicycle, John thought to himself, *you never really forget how to do it.* John hadn't really played the guitar in about twenty years, when he and Maria started dating. His Aria guitar had been stolen from the back of his rental car when he moved into his apartment in Alpharetta back in 2011. John had bought his guitar in circa 1977 for about five hundred dollars, which he had saved during that summer while painting and epoxying massive chemical tanks at the plant in King's Port. Just like virtually all his possessions, they were either stolen, lost, or simply left behind.

In early August, a student at the university moved into the apartment next to John's. His name was Roberto and was in his mid to late twenties and had long, straight black hair well past his shoulders and hailed from Mexico City. Their acquaintance got off to a rough start as Roberto often complained about Molly peeing on the stairs or the foyer down the stairs leading to the gate's exit. John was particularly sensitive about Molly, and anyone who complained about her or treated her unkindly was sure to feel the cold wrath of John's contempt. Roberto was no exception.

But over time, John softened his view of Roberto, and they gradually became good friends. He was intelligent and was close to completing his undergraduate studies in anthropology. He was a very nice and giving person who was fairly fluent in speaking and reading the English language. John lent him a copy of his book, and Roberto liked it, often chiding John for his former escapades. "Such a rebel, that John Headley," Roberto would often jokingly say to John.

With his sixtieth birthday fast approaching in early October, John began carrying on numerous long-distance relationships with women online. There was Elizabeth, who was divorced and living in Chiapas near the northwestern Guatemalan border. She was in her late forties and was a very sweet Mexican lady. She was working on her master's degree in mathematics, and John and she communicated every day. She always sent him a note at night, wishing John peace and sweet dreams.

And there was Connie Couples, a girl John had known from back in his high school and college days, who had moved in with her family across the street in King's Port. She found John on the internet and told him that she had heard that he had written a book, so she bought it and began communicating with John after all those years.

Connie was a beautiful girl from those days, slender and petite with blond hair and blue eyes. She was only two years younger than John yet still a beautiful lady. The last time John had seen Connie was in the summer of 1979, when John had moved back to King's Port from Jacksonville for the summer before graduate school began in the fall. She was a student at East Tennessee State University and had an apartment there in Johnson City. She had always had a crush at John, and he knew it. It was the first time they had touched each other and the first time that they had kissed, after several years of waves from their front yards and occasional small talk. They made love that day for the first time and, likely, the last time. But then again, who knows what life's surprises might be in store.

Another woman also reemerged into John's life at about the same time was none other than Jamie Peters. Jamie and John had always had an attraction for one another but, in over forty years of having known each other, had only found the time to act on it but once. It was really quite remarkable to John that that was the case and probably to her as well. They talked almost daily and relived some of those special moments that they had together, both with great fondness. But they now had become good friends, which had never been the case before. John figured that, at their age, was probably a prerequisite for anything more than that.

And there was beautiful Katia, tall and long legged with blond, golden hair and eyes as blue as the sky. She had just turned twenty-two in late September, and they were still talking about her coming to stay a few days in Chetumal. John doubted it would actually happen and, in a way, thought it probably for the best if it did, indeed, not happen. She was simply too young, and a romantic relationship might scar her psychologically. And probably torment John as well.

Later that same week, Carla had agreed to come over to John's apartment and fix spaghetti with sausage and bacon complimented by salad. John hadn't had spaghetti in almost three years and was really looking forward to it. She said that she would wear her prettiest cotton dress with earrings and put her hair down. It would be just the two of them, a special night.

Carla didn't show up that night, and John was all but certain that he knew why. But irrespective, a person can't make a commitment without keeping it, right? Remember the people of the western Caribbean shores of the Yucatan.

John left her a brief and direct note the next morning on her desk in the salon. It read simply, "As to you, your words are worthless. Goodbye. John."

The next day, content in calling out the obvious, John lay on his bed that afternoon and listened to the wind chimes that Carla had given him and that he had hung by the entrance to his front door. They sang a subtle and peaceful sound as the breeze off the sea had demanded, and he felt good and at peace with himself and life.

But as usually was the case, time heals, and they were back doing whatever it was they were doing before, being a man and a woman.

In mid-August, Katia wrote John and asked him to come and see her in Puerto Vallarta. John responded that Molly would be the problem, and maybe she could come back to Chetumal and he would pay the difference in airfare. They also wrote back and forth about maybe meeting in Mexico City. John was amazed that a beautiful girl like her, so young and pristine, could have such an interest in a man who was nearly, very nearly, sixty. And what an ironic twist of fate, she being from Buenos Aires.

Around the same time, a pretty young girl from Mexico City named Anna moved into the Posada Inn in one of the private rooms. Anna was petite with long golden hair and eyes to match along and a well-toned body. Her eyes were stunningly beautiful of a vivid golden hue. She was there attending the university but spoke very little English. She looked at John with that look; you know, those eyes that have joy in them.

In early September, Olga, John, Miguel, Anna, and the family of Olga's daughter crammed into her minivan for a day trip to Mahahual, a beach resort and once fishing village about sixty miles east or northeast as the crow flies of Chetumal. They were all going to a familial baptism, while John went for a day on the beach.

Mahahual is protected by a reef that is about one hundred meters off shore. It had been originally given by the Mexican government in 1959, in the form of parcels of land, to fishermen who came largely from Veracruz, Acapulco, and Campeche. It officially became part of Mexico and the state of Quintana Roo in 1974. It has now become mainly a tourist village, with pristine beaches and tranquil and the warm aqua blue waters of the Caribbean.

Just before leaving the Inn for Mahahual, Anna grabbed John by both of his biceps and said, "John, you *rico*."

"Hey, Olga, what's *rico*?" John asked.

"She says that you are a rich man," Olga responded.

"Tell her I said that she is *rico* in many blessed ways," John said to Olga with a laugh.

Olga insisted that Miguel sit between them in the third or back, row. She had seen how they were looking at each other. She had become like his grandmother, as she liked to analogize, always watching his interactions with women. John was sure that in this particular case, she would not approve. John wasn't sure if Anna had reached twenty years of life yet.

They flirted like college kids in the van on the way to Mahahual. She would reach around the back of Miguel's neck and tap John on the shoulder and smile the most beautiful of smiles. She had some sort of yogurt-like drink and bottled water and offered John a drink of each. She didn't bother to offer Miguel the same. When they got to the beautiful beach, they walked out into the surf, and she took a picture of John with her cell phone.

Then they, all but John, left for a brief walk to some sort of gathering place for their baptism and party. John relaxed in a chair on the beach and drank *cervazas* for the four hours they were to be gone. It was a spectacular day with a pristine deep-blue sky and nary a cloud could be seen. They were playing wonderful modern Mexican music playing on the large speakers from the adjacent bar and restaurant, which served food and drinks on the beach. The beach wasn't very crowded, and being out of season, it appeared most of the people there were locals or from within Mexico.

John realized that a romantic relationship with Anna was basically out of the question, for obvious reasons. She was only twenty years old, and she lived with Olga, end of story. *But she is nice and fun to be around, so what's the harm in that?* John thought. But then again, John realized there would probably be plenty of harm in that.

John's book had now been out on the market for about two months and, he assumed, was being read by friends and past acquaintances, mainly in King's Port, Atlanta, and Connecticut. Two of John's best friends, Phillip, who now lived with his beautiful family in Austin, and Ronnie, who lived in Zurich with his wonderful family, had read the book and had vastly different responses to it. Phillip didn't really say much to John about the obviously bizarre events that occurred in the last ten years, while Ronnie, on the other hand, talked to John in detail about the events and said that he was very glad and relieved to see that John was through to the other side and was seemingly beyond the chaos and had emerged from the calamity largely unscathed. Ronnie had basically one word of advice, which was "The women are fine, just stay away from the alcohol." The advice was, indeed, obvious and of sound origin.

John had received no responses from either of his ex-wives or Elisa, which was very disappointing to him. He didn't expect to get any responses from Alan or Abby, which he hadn't, but he knew they were all aware of the book.

A Seemingly Innocuous E-mail

With but a week left in September, John received an e-mail from a dating website, just another of many he had received over the years. It was a Latino website, but all communications were in English. But this one was different than the rest, very different. It was well constructed, and the women who were online were right there on the screen, some being the most beautiful and Latino, mainly from Columbia but many, many others from Ecuador, Peru, Chile, Venezuela, Panama, Mexico—yes, Mexico—and Costa Rica.

John thought to himself, *What the hell, why not? I'll upload a few pictures of myself and look at what kind of response I get. I won't actually spend any money. I'll just see what happens.*

John uploaded three pictures of himself—one being from some twelve years before taken of him sitting on the couch by the kitchen back in Alpharetta with Max, Molly's long-since deceased twin brother, and the other two were recent photos taken by Olga and Carla at the Inn and Estetica Carla salon, respectively. These were essentially all the photos he still had of just himself on his laptop.

Within minutes, John began receiving letters from these beautiful girls and women from all over the South and Central Americas. John deemed women under twenty-one years old to be girls, and there were plenty of them.

And these letters weren't cheap. To send a letter, it took ten credits, what amounted to about six dollars. And they got you on the receiving end too. It took an additional ten credits to actually read the letter beyond the first few lines. The website's ownership knew they had laid the golden egg. The temptation was just too great for one to pass up. Some of these women were amazingly beautiful and very forward in their overtures.

One of the first letters John received that day was from a stunning bombshell from Mexico City with blond hair and blue eyes, about five feet and six inches, and 115 pounds and thirty-one years of age. Her name was Erica, and she had never been married. She was a cosmetologist by trade and, as it would turn out, was from Buenos Aires. Her work seemed to be split between the two cities. Fifteen letters from her later, they were planning their union.

Soon to follow were letters from Silvana Alejandra and Solange Alethia, Florencia Luciana, and Georgina, all living in Playa del Carmen. Silvana was a Pilates instructor with dark brown hair with streaks of gold and brown eyes, and she was from Buenos Aires. She was twenty-nine years old and never married.

Stay tuned for more on Silvana Alejandra. Solange was a gorgeous blond with blue eyes but twenty-four years old. She, too, was a sports and pilates instructor. Georgina, a dance instructor, was a tall and slender beauty with brunette hair and brown eyes. She had never been married either. Later it would turn out that she too was from Argentina. She wrote a letter to John from there, telling him when she would be returning. John found it amazing how many of these beautiful women had never been married but, he guessed, men in South and Central America probably weren't as respectful and motivated career-wise to satisfy these lovely creatures. *What an opportunity*, John thought. *These women want to meet me, and for the first time in ten years, I'm ready and willing to do so.*

By his sixtieth birthday, John was in regular contact with about ten or twelve of these beautiful women, and a couple of girls, and had received well over one thousand e-mails. John couldn't read the vast majority of the letters; he simply didn't have the money, or time for that matter, to do so. It was truly astonishing to John that there seemed to be so much interest in him in this part of the world but realized it probably had a lot to do with being American, having blond hair and blue eyes, having been a financial executive, and finally, having written a book that they could see on Amazon and hear about it on YouTube.

There was Estafania, a twenty-five-year-old of Italian descent, a lady with a face and body of a goddess. She was from Medellin and was an internet web designer who had told John early on that she wanted him—only him. And there was Lina Maria, twenty-four and so much more, and a gorgeous brunette from Bogota. One of her pictures was of her sitting cross-legged on a marble floor in only a bra and panties, her long black hair draped around her shoulders and back. And Paula Andrea, who was also from Bogota, who was as pretty as any woman John had ever seen.

And then there was Damaris Juletsy, a stunning creature of twenty years of age and from Ecuador. Her pictures in the surf of the ocean in her bikini were so nice. Damaris wrote John four or five letters a day, very few of which John had been able to read. He felt really badly about it, this young and naïve girl of such exquisite beauty seemingly smitten with John, and he didn't have the heart nor the money or, one might say, the decency to ask her to stop writing to him for her own good; to tell her that he wouldn't be right for her.

And then there was Yulieth Vanessa, twenty-one years of age and certainly one of the prettiest girls John had ever laid his eyes on, with long, shimmering black hair and piercing black eyes and a body to die for. In her most recent letter to John, she said that she had gotten her visa, and she was coming to him in December to be his Christmas present and wanted to stay forever. Simply unbelievable it was to John.

And then there was Maria Paula, who, ironically, was also from Buenos Aires but lived in Mexico City and performed dance routines in the circus. She also gave pole dancing lessons to the girls of the gentlemen's clubs scene. She was twenty-eight years old with long black hair and dark brown eyes and, yes, you guessed it, a body that was to die for, and she had seemingly fallen in love with John from afar, and perhaps, he too with her. They wrote to one another often and also planned to meet in the near future.

Last, but certainly not least, there was Maria Belen, a thirty-year-old model from Guadalajara, with long, flowing black hair and brown eyes and the body and face of a goddess. She came to the game late, but better late than never from John's perspective. John was shocked that she had chosen him, and she pretty much said so much in her second letter to him that she was happy that they had made a connection, and she wanted to pursue it further. She told John that she had no interest in anyone else on the site.

John felt that he had created a mess for himself. They all probably thought from his bio that, being a recent author of a book and a former executive in the insurance and reinsurance industries, that money was not a problem. It was a huge problem. John kept telling himself, "You can't play, John, with just what you have today."

There were others, so many others, that it was hard to keep track of them for John—or to choose, if one were to have to—among them. Some of the girls also, especially the South American women, liked to try to catch John online late at night for a live chat and touch themselves while they wrote to John and looked at his pictures. John often wondered why that propensity existed with the South American women. They would then touch themselves and describe to John in explicit detail what they were doing with him and how wonderful their orgasms felt. John often wondered to himself, *Could they really be doing that? That's quite a display of skillful dexterity, if so. But you know, John, there is usually a minute or two of digital silence toward the end of your conversations.* Like so many other times in recent years, John felt as though he were living his life through the lenses of a camera; a mere onlooker to this other man's reality.

Soon after this website had contacted John, an apparent sister or affiliate website featuring Eastern European women contacted John, and he put up the same pictures and general bio information to this site, and within two weeks, John had received almost one thousand five hundred e-mails from women in Ukraine, Serbia, Bulgaria, Greece, Portugal, and Spain. They were teachers, doctors, lawyers, journalists, you name it, and most of them were highly educated a fluent in English. But it was funny because sometimes there would be a twenty-year-old student or the like, who was a finance expert or doctor or lawyer—go figure. And so many were absolutely gorgeous. Many were models in Kiev or Odessa or Luhansk or Lisbon, or even one from Moscow and one from St. Petersburg, and they would write many times, puzzled why John wouldn't respond to them. They clearly could have virtually any man in the world that they wanted. *Why me?* John often wondered. And through all these e-mails, from what John could tell, not one of them ever asked if one of his pictures might have been taken quite a few years before. Amazing.

In the meantime, Olga had gone with John to be his translator for an initial consultation with an orthopedic surgeon regarding his lower back, what had now been a major problem for well over forty years. John brought with him x-rays that had been taken at the Karl Huesner hospital in Belize City in May, which John had then intended to use to file a disability claim through the US Embassy in Belmopan. He now had contacted the US Consulate in Playa del Carmen, who were expecting his visit regarding the filing, as well as to renew his passport, which was to expire at the end of November. The doctor looked at the x-rays and confirmed what John knew that his L3 and L4 vertebrae were a mess and that, for a complete and proper diagnosis, prescribed an MRI to be done at the local public hospital.

The MRI was then scheduled for November 3, and with that in hand, the doctor would then write a diagnosis and recommendation, which John knew would be surgery because he had gone through this with two other doctors in 1983 and 2001. The MRI would cost John six thousand pesos, or about $310, so he had to wait until November to have the money available for it. John wondered why he had waited so long to do this, given all the financial misery he had suffered through in the past several years. Part of it was laziness and part of it was due to generally not having the money to pay for the MRI.

Given that John would be in Playa del Carmen shortly after the third, he had made plans with both Silvana Alejandra and Solange Alethia to get together when he was there, thinking that one would kind of disappear in the meantime. Neither did, and both were excited about his visit and fully expecting to meet with him. John would have to choose between them, or be creative and kill two birds with one stone, so to speak. This dilemma he would have to resolve sooner than later.

It was certainly hard to imagine that this was the same John Headley that Olga had taken to the hospital less than two months before. John was suffering from malnutrition, acute insomnia, and depression. He was put on an IV over the night, as Olga had served as his translator with the doctor, who spoke no English.

The next day, John was fed two meals and given a prescription for his insomnia. He had again lost much weight and found it difficult to maintain his balance, but he was released anyway that afternoon. And it was Olga who had, once again, spared John from what could have ended in a really bad way. She, this woman that John had only known a mere two months.

These episodes seemed to happen now and then; they came unannounced and uninvited but came nonetheless. John was sure that it had to do with a need to bring closure to his estrangement, or maybe a better word would be absence, from Alan and Abby, closure that he so desperately needed.

It was now early October, and John was visiting Olga on the afternoon and day before his sixtieth birthday, where he met two young men who were senior college students at the university in Mexicali and who were in Chetumal to give a presentation at the local university on linguistics. They were very friendly and both were very smart and fluent in English. Joni, the elder of the two, was twenty-seven and was the more experienced of the two in the art of presentations and with the streets of life in general. His cohort, Andy, was born and raised in Mexicali, whereas Joni had been born and raised in Mesa, Arizona. He was attending the university in Mexicali because it was so much cheaper than in the States.

They had learned that the next day was John's birthday, and they had already made plans to make a day trip to Mahahual for a little rest and relaxation after their morning presentation. They asked John if he would like to come along with them, to which John said yes, thinking what better way to spend his sixtieth birthday than on the beautiful beaches of Mahahual.

John met Joni and Andy the next day shortly after lunch, and they had already secured a taxi driver for the duration of the day. For the driver's services, it would cost a total of a mere thousand pesos, or about fifty dollars, which included gas and his *dormi* time while they would enjoy the playa and the beautiful waters of the Caribbean.

They passed through Bacalar on the way, which was only a short thirty or so kilometers north of Chetumal. Bacalar was the lake of many colors and boundless depths, to which many tourists and locals alike came to see.

They then quickly headed north and then ultimately to the east and southeast to traverse the Bay of Chetumal, as there was no bridge that crossed the bay, which would have made the journey half the distance. As they rode along, John couldn't help but get a sense of surrealism; yet another out-of-body kind of feeling. *Here I am*, John thought to himself, *going to spend my sixtieth birthday at a beach I knew absolutely nothing about a mere six weeks ago, with two college kids from Mexicali. And I live here in Mexico, in Chetumal, the state of Quintana Roo. How has all this come to be?*

The afternoon was an unforgettable treat, served up with grilled local fish and beers and a margarita, gratis, and a front row seat at a table on the Caribbean. Joni and Andy made for great company, and John learned a lot about their generation and what made them tick, so to speak, like what music they liked and what they planned to do next in life. Joni planned to go to graduate school in either Germany or Canada, where the school would presumably be free. Andy was a music enthusiast and was especially enthralled by the hippie era of the sixties and the associated music. And Joni and Andy learned about how John had written his first book and how his second book was coming along and very likely to end on that very day. They heard about John's life as a financial executive in the insurance industry, and they learned about John's views on politics and life in general, and what it all could possibly mean. *Who knows?* John concluded. It was, ultimately, a day in the life, nothing more and nothing less, but memorable nonetheless.

Well, John thought to himself, *I've cashed in all my chips for my first sixty years of my life—a life which has been filled with much joy and pleasure and devastating hurt and sorrow. All I have to show for it are three beautiful children and one that left this world far too soon.*

Belize had been a story of survival. John had truly forgotten that love existed. He now knew that it did, he just didn't know where. John felt content in his own skin for the first time in a decade, his last mission being to be reunited, if only for a brief time, with his children. He was confident that would come soon.

John couldn't help but think about the past decade and how it had seemingly been stolen, or taken away, from him, and he was intent on getting it back, intent on living those ten years all over again. And nobody in his new life would be the wiser for it.

"But your and my heart still beats. I often wonder why, what's the point of it all. I thought I knew the answer at one point, but not anymore. In the end, I never had any idea, nor do you. And after all this, do you want to know the truth? There is no universal truth, only what we think is such." *All the truths in the world add up to one big lie.*

I could be beautiful, but I'm not. I could make you happy, but that won't happen in the end. I could be a part of you, but I'm not, I'm here alone. I could be content, but I'm not. I could have many, but I have none. I could look at you, but I won't. I run and hide, and I'm here, hiding, ashamed. So where does this leave us, you might ask? Nowhere, but where we are, of that I'm sure.

I'm wound up tight
I'm out of range
I used to care but
Things have changed

And I can't conclude without a word about Olga, who without I would not be who I am or feeling life as it is—I was totally numb to it, the whole of it. She gave me life, life again, and for that, I'm so grateful and alive again. It's still a struggle sometimes, as I suspect it is for all.

I hurt myself today
To see if I still feel
I focus on the pain
The only thing that's real
The needle tears a hole
The old familiar sting
Try to kill it all away
But I remember everything

What have I become
My sweetest friend
Everyone I know goes away in the end
And you could have it all
My empire of dirt
I will let you down
I will make you hurt

I wear this crown of thorns
Upon my liar's chair
Full of broken thoughts
I cannot repair
Beneath the stains of time
The feelings disappear
You are someone else
I am still right here

What have I become
My sweetest friend
Everyone I know goes away in the end
And you could have it all
My empire of dirt
I will let you down
I will make you hurt

If I could start again
A million miles away
I would keep myself
I would find a way
(*"Hurt"* by Johnny Cash)

Epilogue

An Ending and a New Beginning

So after all that had happened in the past year, and throughout his entire life, John realized that all the hundreds of relationships he had had with women were episodes or love songs—some short, some long, but all inevitably with the same outcome. They, and he, were all ships passing in the night in this journey of life. Some for a while, others for a brief interlude, but each one unforgettable nonetheless.

> *You're just a memory*
> *And it used to mean so much to me.*

They shared love, lust, sex, happiness, and some, sadness, but each would not forget the other, for it is these memories that make us who we are and create the mold of a person, neither perfect or imperfect, who is trying to live life as best they can, realizing that life is a fast-moving train, and we can't jump off at the next stop. Life must, and will, go on with or without us. We, the man and the woman, and our shared moments of embracement in this world continue to make us who we are and are a reflection of life itself, and the lives of all men and women. Different as night and day but intertwined so inextricably so as not to be able to live life fully and completely without the other.

> Is it getting any better
> Or do you feel the same

Will it make it easier on you now
If you've got someone to blame

You said one love
One life
When it's one need
In the night
One love we get to share it
It leaves you baby if you don't care for it

Did I disappoint you
Or leave a bad taste in your mouth
You act like you never had love
And you want me to go without

Well it's too late
Tonight
To drag the past out
Into the light
We're one but we're not the same
We get to carry each other
Carry each other
One

Have you come here for forgiveness?
Have you come to raise the dead?
Have you come here to play Jesus
To the lepers in your head?

Did I ask too much
More than a lot?
You gave me nothing now
It's all I've got
We're one but we're not same

              (*"One"* by U2)

This is my love song to each and every one of you. Thank you for the memories, as they are all that I have. Godspeed.

> I caught sight of my reflection
> I caught it in the window
> I saw the darkness in my heart
> I saw the signs of my undoing
>
> In the blood of Eden
> Lie the woman and the man
> With the man in the woman
> And the woman in the man
> We wanted the union
> Of the union of the woman
> The woman and the man
> (*"The Blood of Eden"* by Peter Gabriel)

Wait. What's that bright light on the horizon? Ah, I see, it's another ship in the night, passing by soon. We'll see what sort of unexpected interlude that it might bring.

John looked out the window at the Aki sign and realized it had stayed illuminated for long past its usual time. And then it went dark, suddenly and unexpectedly, hoping to live again and emerge anew for yet another day.

About the Author

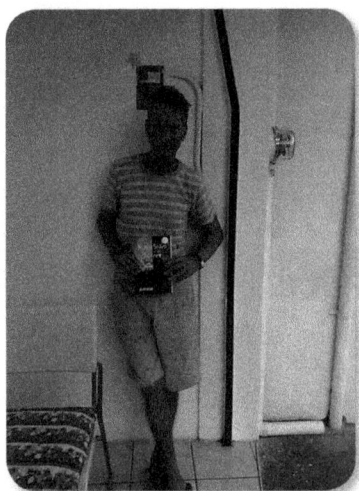

Alan currently lives in Chetumal, Mexico, on the beautiful Chetumal Bay of the Caribbean, which is on the Belize border. It is there where this book was written and is a sequel to his first book, *On Both Sides of the Street*.

Alan graduated with a master's degree in accountancy from the University of Tennessee, received his certification as a public accountant and embarked on a career in the insurance and reinsurance industries that spanned over twenty years. Financial management positions led him various cities, including Kansas City, Atlanta, and culminating as the chief financial officer and executive vice president of the North American operations one of the largest life and health reinsurance companies in the world. During this ten-year period, he lived in Stamford, Connecticut, and worked both there and in Armonk, New York.

Personal tragedies would lead to his premature departure from the financial world and into a life of uncertainty, and in some instances, a life of survival. He moved to Belize in 2013 from Stuart, Florida, in a "desperate escape," as he coined it, and from there to Chetumal in the summer of 2016.

Viva, Mexico!

CPSIA information can be obtained
at www.ICGtesting.com
Printed in the USA
LVHW052009220720
661200LV00005B/296

9 781642 146769